Cc

By John Turner

Ronnie—
Never stop
pooping!

John Turner
June 2014

Published by Goat House Books
P.O. Box 1031
Skaneateles, NY 13152
www.goathousebooks.com

Published in the United States of America

ISBN: 1494968037
ISBN-13: 978-1494968038

First edition, Goat House Books printing, January 2014

TABLE OF CONTENTS

1. INTRODUCTION

I want you to do me a favor: after you've decided you'd like to keep this book around for a while, go put it on the back of your toilet. (Kindle users, you're just gonna have to figure this one out for yourselves.)

Once I started putting this collection together, I realized that the amount of time it takes to read a story—five minutes or so, depending on which story you're reading—is about the same as the time it takes to, ah... "drop the kids off at the pool," in the parlance of our times. Plus, I hope these stories will give you some reasons to consider your place in the universe, and I truly believe we humans do our best thinking on the shitter. (The old "garbage in, garbage out" adage. Or something like that.)

That being said, let me tell you a little bit about where the universe has taken me: I grew up in a small town in Mississippi, then got my college degree in Acting/Music. In 1999, I moved to upstate New York to work for an educational theatre company. By this time, I was a full-fledged alcoholic. Three years later, in May 2002, I was beaten almost to death by a guy I'd met in a bar. I suffered a traumatic brain injury in the attack and I was in a coma for nearly a month. After that I no longer had the physical capabilities to perform, so I became a writer. (Yet my alcoholism continued—worsened, in fact.) Over the next 10 years or so, I spiraled slowly downward: I got engaged, then my fiancée left me; I landed a great job as a journalist for the local paper, only to be fired a couple of years later; I was evicted from my home...every one of those things happened as a direct result of my addiction.

In January of 2012, I came to Key West, Fla., because one of the only friends I had left lives here. By then, I figured (and sort of hoped) I'd end up drinking myself to death. Guess what? That didn't happen. Instead, I found the rooms of Alcoholics Anonymous, and I've been clean/sober since March 26, 2012. And my sobriety has finally—*finally*—given me the presence of mind and the courage to compile this here tome.

Now a word or three about the following stories: About 18 months after my injury in 2002, I was suffering from a deep depression. I couldn't work, or sleep, or eat...I wasn't even sure why I was alive anymore. But my mom had just bought me a computer, so over the course of about 10 days (and a ton of tears) I wrote the title story, "Confessions of a Gimp." In writing it, I exorcised some demons, had some laughs, and found a new purpose for living.

Over the next decade, I wrote a story every few months, when a particularly powerful memory struck me or an anecdote-worthy event occurred. And these stories are...oh, I'll say 85 percent true. The events I describe all happened—I didn't fictionalize those at all—but I've taken a few liberties with dialogue and other details. (The one exception is "The Frankie Jean Lewis Trip." Written mere days after my family and I had visited the Jerry Lee Lewis Museum in Ferriday, Louisiana, everything in the story happened exactly as I describe. Hell, I'm not talented enough to make that kind of shit up!)

You'll notice I included the year(s) each story covers in its title. That's because I think of these tales as "snapshots" of events that have occurred during the 43 years I've been alive. Some are like Polaroids, others like a series of time-lapse shots. Let me say this, too: my philosophy and perspective have changed quite a lot over the past decade, but I've left the stories as they were when I originally wrote them, because they represent exactly where my head was at the time.

And being the lifelong music junkie I am, I've actually made a soundtrack to accompany this book. After the title of each story I've written the title of the song that best supplements the tale. Some are tunes that came out around the time the story was composed; others inspire me in the same way the story does; still others just seem to fit the narrative.

OK, that's enough for now—let's do this. Have fun!

—Key West, Fla., November 2013

2. THE BLIND LEADING THE STUPID (2005)

(previously published in
Breath and Shadow in 2007)

(Soundtrack: ARETHA FRANKLIN—
"Chain of Fools")

It was the performance of a lifetime.

All my acting training, the dozens of roles I'd portrayed, the thousands of plays I'd performed in....all of it had led up to this. My *piece de resistance*. My entire life's work had been preparation for this one...split...second.

Was I ready? Did I have the balls for it?

You'd better believe I did.

I was rushing through Atlanta's Hartsfield International Airport (well, if you want to call my jerky imitation of Pinocchio "rushing"), after being dumped off a scant few hundred yards from my gate by the Woop-Woop Cart. (Those are the carts with sirens that transport the aged and infirm through larger airports; the drivers are crazed with panic, and apparently the loud "woop-woop" sound the carts make causes absolutely no one to move out of the way.)

The plane to Atlanta was just a shuttle, so we'd disembarked out on the tarmac. The sun had just bloomed over the horizon when we touched down, so I put on my sunglasses as we left the plane. In my haste to reach my next gate in time, I didn't give them another thought.

My cane, one of those generic chrome four-footed jobs, was missing a rubber bumper, so it made an annoying "clack, clack" as I jerked my way towards the gate. I hobbled as fast as I could up to the ticket counter.

"Has the....plane....left yet?" Breathless, I held out my boarding pass.

"No, you're right on time, Mr. Turner," the attendant replied sweetly. After she'd run my pass over the laser, she grabbed my hand as she put the ticket back into my grip. *Weird. Why did she...?*

Seconds later, another attendant popped out (of the wall? Where did these folks come from?), stepped over to me and put my arm through hers.

"Come on. I'll give you a hand," she said. "The plane's still boarding, so we have plenty of time. Now...coming to a doorway...there's a little step down...there you go..."

Suddenly, I understood: The cane, my limp, I still had my shades on.... I let out an involuntary laugh. They thought I was blind.

The realization hit me like a shock-wave. *Are they really that stupid? My cane isn't the least bit white...and how do they think I made it all the way to the gate unassisted? Lord.*

I had to make a snap decision: Should I

tell them? Or did I want to keep it going?

I was an actor, after all. This would be my own personal Oscar moment. I figured I'd play it for all it was worth, throw in all the idiotic stereotypes, and see if someone caught on.

Hearing me chortle, the attendant said, "What's funny?"

"Huh? Oh...oh, nothing. You wouldn't believe it if I told you." *You're looking at her face...don't look at her face!!*

In the early days of my acting career, long before my brain injury, I'd played the blind guy in *Butterflies Are Free* at the local community theater. It's a play about a blind kid, Don, who finds the guts to move out on his own, away from his domineering mother. He moves into an apartment next door to a saucy piece of meat named Jill, and she and Don pretty much boff on the couch for the rest of the play.

I'd thought Jill must be pretty desperate to date a guy who couldn't see her–remember, this was years before I became disabled myself—but the actress who played her was named Lhay Whiting, and she was beautiful. (Yes, Lhay. Pronounced like "lay." How could I resist?)

I'd visited a school for the blind to prepare for the role, and I remembered how the blind people I'd met just look in the general direction of people they talk to. So as we walked down the jetway, I focused on a spot on the wall just beside the attendant's head. I pasted on a huge, shit-eating grin and nodded as if I had no idea what she was talking about. (And it's funny how people barely hid their looks of sympathy; I could see it in their eyes: *Oh, this poor kid...*)

The sympathy masks continued when I entered the plane. The attendant exclaimed, "This is Mr. Turner! He's in...?" She looked at me, forgetting that I couldn't read the boarding pass (which I almost did anyway). After a moment, she started and looked at the pass.

"12D! It's 12D. Have a safe flight." As she turned to scurry away, the look of relief on her face was too much. I dug my nails into my palms to keep from laughing as I shuffled around to face the flight crew.

"Misterrr Turrnerrrrrr!! Right this way..." A beautiful black attendant stepped forward and grabbed my arm. As she pulled me down the aisle towards my seat, I nervously glanced at the faces of the passengers already seated. *Was I believable? Could I pull it off?* The looks on their faces said I could; some people gave me looks of pity, while others just stared.

Okay, here we are...12D," she said, gently guiding me into the seat with her hand. "Here, let me take your luggage for you." She reached towards my carry-on bag.

"Ummmmm....can I keep it with me?" I asked the seat in front of me.

"Well..." She tried stuffing it under the

seat, but it was way too big, so she faked it. "I guess you can. I'll just put it under this seat." She guided my hand to it so I'd know where it was. I could tell without looking that it stuck halfway into the aisle. "All set?"

Oh jeez, I'm onto something here. I said to the seat, "Yes, thanks. Can you...I might need some help with the snacks...?"

"Of course we can!! We'll be serving them after the plane takes off."

I settled in for the flight. Airplanes are great for people-watching, so I began scanning the cabin for other interesting souls. Then I remembered: *You're friggin blind, idiot!* I quickly unfocused my eyes and, reapplying my "I'm blind and maybe feebleminded" grin, cast my gaze back on the seat in front of me.

I was proud of my performance so far...but all the special treatment had me confused and a little nervous. *Why the heck are they being so damn nice? I seriously doubt they treat all blind passengers like this. Do they know? Is all the special attention their way of setting me up?*

I finally realized that there was no turning back. *What's the worst that can happen? It's not like they're gonna throw me off the plane.*

After we took off, I began to "look" around the cabin again by doing a Ray Charles-type head swing. The other travelers were as diverse as an ACLU poster. Behind the sunglasses, I was able to really study people— their mannerisms, the way they shifted uncomfortably in their seats. I also noticed that folks would steal only quick glances at me, like they were afraid I would catch them looking. This puzzled me even more. *Am I obviously a fake? Or are they really that ignorant? Just don't break. You're doing fine, Stevie Wonder.*

We leveled off, and it was snack time. When the attendant reached me, she put down my tray table herself and positioned my hand on my soda. Then she opened my minuscule bag of pretzels and settled them in my free hand. "There you go," she said. I was close to losing it.

"Thanks." *You can do it. Think about the time you started the mower after a newborn kitten had crawled onto the blade.* That seemed to sober me a bit. I popped the pretzels into my mouth with machine-gun rapidity and drank my soda in three gulps.

My giggles stifled for the time being, I put on my headphones and dozed until we began our descent. I again marveled at the way they were treating me. *Boy, if this is how blind people are really treated, I'm gonna do this every time I fly.*

During my semi-slumber, an idea began brewing in the part of my brain that controls nastiness. By the time we were strapped in for landing, I'd talked myself into it.

Seeing my grin, the black attendant teased, "Now what's so darn funny?" I sat up, startled.

"Wha...oh, it was something I was listening to." I put my headphones into my bag.

"You like comedy, huh? You know, I saw that new movie with Tyler Perry, where he plays a woman? I laughed..." She droned on and on, but I wasn't listening. I was absorbed by the potential fallout after my little stunt. *What if they arrest me? They won't. Just do it and get out.*

We landed without incident, but a warm ball was forming in my stomach over what I was about to do.

As we taxied to the gate, the attendant gave her "Welcome to..." speech, grinning broadly at me the whole time. Towards the end, she winked. *Wait a minute. Why would she do that? Does she know—*

The "Fasten Seatbelt" light blinked off with a "ding," prompting the eighty or so passengers to rise in unison. As they slowly filed towards the door, I waited, my heart racing. *What now? Even if she does know, the others might not. Just do it.*

After the last passenger had shuffled by, I sprang into action. I whipped off my sunglasses, stood and put my bag on my shoulder. I strolled down the aisle beaming, making sure to make eye contact with each member of the flight crew.

They stood and stared, and as I approached them, their faces were like slot machines: disbelief, rage, joy, and back to disbelief again.

No one said a word, though, as I shuffled through the door into the jetway.

****

I'm not blind. I have a brain injury, which causes me to move and talk slowly. I have no mental damage. I'm still the same charming, goofy, sneaky, malicious bastard I've always been. The fact that the airline people assumed I was blind because I moved and talked funny–*and* I happened to be wearing sunglasses—is their mistake, not mine. And in making that mistake, they picked a guy who would take it to the next level. That's it.

But perhaps in taking it to that next level, I was *too* good, considering all the extra attention I got. My disability doesn't normally gain much notice, save for the occasional holding of a door. Why, then, was I treated so well when I appeared to be blind, too? It's a thought that still perplexes me.

As I exited the jetway into the terminal, I looked for the flight attendant who had winked at me. I just had to know whether she'd found me out, and I prepared myself for either a good laugh or a harsh scolding.

Sadly, I didn't see her, so I was doomed never to know if she had indeed discovered my secret. Even so, I walked through the terminal with a near-spring in my step, and I was still giggling to myself when I left the airport parking lot.

INTERLUDE:
How Are You Feeling?

Because of my disability, a lot of people do me favors, like holding the door for me or offering me a hand up or down the steps.

And while I'm grateful for the help, some folks are just so ignorant, thoughtless, or uninformed that they don't know when to stop.

It happens about once a day. Someone will get right in my face and say, "HEY BUDDY!! HOW ARE YOU FEELING??"

Christ. How are YOU feeling? And I think some people think that since I'm physically disabled, I must also have a single-digit IQ. Just the other day, my neighbor was standing on the steps as I shuffled down them.

"Be careful. You're gonna make it!" he said.

I didn't know what else to do, so I asked him if he could carry me the 50 feet or so to my apartment door. And even though he's in his seventies, and has a gimpy leg himself, he said he would. I told him I was kidding, but he didn't appreciate the joke.

3. THE ERRANT STREAM (1999)

(Soundtrack: BEASTIE BOYS—"Slow and Low")

I never would've believed that peeing on myself would change my entire life.

The fact that a single stream of urine would hold my fate, my future, my very *existence* in its pale yellow flow....well, that just gives me the shivers, in an Eastern-type, metaphysical sort of way. The events set off by my misguided stream altered everything. I moved halfway across the country and embarked on a new career, and my life has completely changed since.

During the lean years before my bathroom debacle, I was kicking around the small city near my hometown, working at a video store and crying myself to sleep. Having received my bachelor's degree in acting from a nearby university, I was in career hell—a familiar place to more than a few theatre majors. Self-righteous as I am, I wasn't overly concerned; I simply figured that the correct people hadn't yet discovered my brilliance. I only needed to be in the right place at the right time.

Little did I know that the right place and time was a public bathroom in Greensboro, North Carolina one day in the spring of 1999.

There was a theatre conference that year

at a Greensboro convention center, tucked into the foothills of the Smoky Mountains, which I had decided to attend. And why not? I wasn't winning any Oscars working at Blockbuster. So I signed up and made the trip.

The conference was huge. In addition to dozens of workshops, speakers, and how-to classes daily, 1,200 actors auditioned for 200 theatre companies over the course of three days. I was lucky enough to audition the morning of the first day—I was number 52.

The process was long and nerve-wracking. Performers were divided into groups of twenty, and each group lined up and prepared in a "holding room" before they went into the theater. (And let me tell you, the holding room resembled a gathering of schizophrenics. Actors would walk around ostensibly warming up, barking out "Ha! Ha! Haaaaaaa...." or hissing, "Ppppppssshhh." A fly on the wall would've been scared to death.)

When you went into the theater, you sat in chairs along the wall, while 300 some-odd producers stared at you. As you went up to perform—90 seconds, including a song—you walked up a few stairs, then through the wings onto the stage. You did your thing, then went off the same way and back to your chair. It was an intense few minutes, no doubt.

But I was ready. The *Rocky* theme was running through my head as I made my way into the holding room. My tummy lurched a little, but I just mistook it for nerves.

That was mistake number one.

I sat quietly as the others did their Tourette's impressions. My stomach was now boiling but good, and I began to wonder if I shouldn't make the mad dash to the bathroom. I had sudden flashes of just what would happen if I...uh, had an accident while waiting to perform. That sealed the deal, so to speak.

I stood with care and walked stiff-legged to the door. The boy working the door for the convention eyed me carefully, and just as I began to speak, a cramp ripped through my body.

"I need to–" *Groooooowwwwwlll.* The kid immediately understood.

"Over there." He pointed, and I was *gone.* As I half-ran toward the men's room, I glanced over my shoulder. The kid was watching me with disgust, no doubt because of the tremendous fart I'd just laid.

Oh my God, I thought as I rushed to a stall. I believe that in times such as this, your body knows what's about to happen, because I could barely hold it in. The turtle was peeking out of its shell, as they say.

I pulled down my pants, plopped down on the toilet, and let loose with a torrent of feces. I figured that while I was there, I might as well pee, too.

Mistake number two.

See, sometimes when a guy sits too

quickly on the toilet, his little buddy gets caught on the lip of the bowl. And that's what happened to me. Before I knew it, I'd wet the entire back of my khakis—my brand new, immaculately pressed khakis.

Oooooooh nooooooooooooo!!!

I finished and pulled up my pants. My ass was soaked, no two ways about it. I could feel drops of urine rolling down my legs.

I almost started crying as my brain hit overdrive: *What to do, what to do, what the HELL do I do??* I knew we'd be called into the theater any second, so I had to get back into the holding room *now*. I did the only thing I could think of. I untucked my button-down shirt and pulled it down as far as I could. I looked over my shoulder at my butt, and I could already see the stain spreading. My shirt, of course, having been tucked in, was horribly wrinkled from the waist down.

Oh well. It's only my life. I figured I'd go with it. I had a Bachelor of Fine Arts degree, dammit, and I wasn't going to let some piddling little pee-soaked hiney ruin my chances. It was now or never.

I strode back to the holding room, as confident as a movie star. Luckily, my seat was near the door, so I side-stepped to my seat with my back against the wall, garnering a few inquisitive stares from the other actors.

As I sat in my pee-puddle, I recalled a fact I'd learned in high school physics: *Friction creates heat.* Bingo! I started rubbing my butt back and forth on the plastic seat, trying to be as subtle as possible. The actor sitting next to me cut her eyes at me. *Does she know? Do I reek of pee?* It didn't matter. She wasn't going to hire me, either way.

After what seemed like only seconds, a convention worker barked, "Okay, let's line up!" *Here we go. You can do it. Dry ass, dry ass, dry ass!* As we filed into the theater, 300 heads turned as one to look at us. I was encouraged by the fact that the path to our chairs was against the wall, so I side-stepped again, hugging my butt against it. The huge, desperate grin on my face gained a few return smiles from the producers.

I was the twelfth actor to audition, so I had twenty minutes or so to continue my ass-rubbing. As I ground my butt back and forth, I tried not to vomit, both from the smell and from my electrified nerves.

And then it was time. As I strode onstage, an eerie calm came over me. *It's almost like the old cliche of everyone being naked. Except instead of them being nude, they're watching a guy perform with a urine-covered butt.* Never mind the fact that I smelled like a homeless person–they weren't going to hire me for my aroma.

My performance was *awesome.* I had nothing to lose, so I went for it like I never had before. I slipped a little at the end, because when I took a breath before the last long note of the song, my nostrils were filled with the stench of a New York City subway.

Then, I was somehow back in my seat. I must have been successful in fooling them, too, because I received more than thirty requests for callback interviews. And by the time we left the theater, my butt was dry as a bone.

A couple of weeks later, there was a message waiting for me when I got home from work. An educational theatre company in upstate New York wanted to hire me. Two months later, I was on a train bound for Syracuse, the first of many changes I think I owe to that errant stream. In a bizarre way, it gave me the courage and confidence to just not give a damn during that audition. My life hasn't been the same since.

INTERLUDE: If the Shoe Fits, Eat it

So I was at the bus stop having a smoke while I waited for the next bus, when a cute girl who looked to be about five months pregnant came down the sidewalk.

She stopped when she got to me. "Hey, you wouldn't happen to have an extra cigarette, would you?"

The shred of morals I had left answered, "You know, I don't feel comfortable giving a cigarette to a pregnant lady."

She looked confused for a second, then both humiliation and irritation flickered across her face. "But....but I'm not pregnant."

My eyes ran down her body, and a second look told me that no, she just loved her some ravioli. Or beer. (Or both.)

I felt so bad I gave her two.

4. THE TALE OF JERRY LEWIS (1981)

(Soundtrack: JOHN FOGERTY—
"Centerfield")

No, not *that* Jerry Lewis. This Jerry Lewis played on my little league baseball team when I was 11. A 10-year-old bean-pole, he looked like what Alfred E. Neuman would've looked like if he'd grown up in rural Alabama.

You see, Jerry was country. And by country, I mean working on a farm your whole life. Living in a one-room house. And bringing your whole family to ballgames on a tractor.

Yes. His family would hitch a flatbed trailer onto their old International Harvester, and the whole family—six or eight more bean-poles of various ages—would spread out like bacon strips in a pan and sun themselves on the trip to the ballfield. And if I hadn't seen this, I wouldn't have believed it either: Sometimes their mom would ride side-saddle on the front fender. Holy jeez, the *Deliverance* theme stayed in my head for years.

Our coach was a psychiatrist in his mid-forties, a Marine, German, named Dr. Heigel. (Later, we would joke: "There goes Doctor Heigel! Sieg HEIL!!") His two sons, Andy and Tommy, were on the team. They were...well, they were both State Spelling Bee champions. No lie.

We were terrible. I was the catcher,

mainly because I was the only one who wouldn't dive out of the way when a pitch crossed the plate.

Either Andy or Tommy would pitch, and the other would play first. We'd lose games 17-1, and Dr. Heigel (Sieg Heil!) would say, "Good job, guys! It's not a shutout, so that's much better than last week!"

Jerry Lewis played right field–the Pluto of little league ball. He was right-handed, but he didn't have a baseball glove. Dr. Heigel (Sieg Heil!) lent him a spare one, but his sons were both left-handed, so the glove was on Jerry's throwing hand.

Since it was the only time he ever touched the ball, folks loved to watch Jerry warm up. He'd catch the ball in his right, pull off the glove with his left, snatch the ball with his right again, and throw. After he got good at it, it took him only three or four seconds–if he didn't drop the ball during the exchange.

One Saturday afternoon, the sun was beating down, and it was a perfect day for baseball. The field smelled of newly-cut grass as I ran onto the field to warm up. We actually had a chance to win, too; our opponents, the Edwards Eagles, hadn't won a game either.

Then, I heard it: the Lewises were coming.

The tractor purred as it came over the hill. I spotted Jerry first, in his feverishly white uniform. Then I saw his mom on the fender, and the rest of the brood finally came into focus. But there was something else: a weird pink...blob...

Is that...is that a pig?

It was. As the tractor rolled closer, I saw it: a young sow on a leash, proud and almost grinning, like she was as happy as a pig in...well, you know. Everyone stared as they pulled up, but the Lewises just smiled back, as if they were taking their dog out for an afternoon walk. The pig gave a "Squeeeeeeee!" just to let us know she knew she was the center of attention.

Jerry ran onto the field and lined up right in front of me, but I couldn't take my eyes off the pig, who trotted along at the feet of Jerry's sister Bobbie.

"Look out!!" everyone screamed. I dove out of the way as a ball thrown by Jerry went *pffffit* past my ear.

'Soah-rey," Jerry said. "I thought you was ready."

"So...so that's your pig, huh?"

'Yay-up."

"It have a name?"

"Oh. That there's Puddin."

Hm. Puddin the Pig. Have mercy.

I just stared as Jerry did his glove-shuffle. *Wow. Am I dreaming?* I looked over at Puddin. *No, not dreaming.* As if answering my thoughts, Bobbie asked her, "Are you huuuuun-gry?" "SQUEEEEEEEEEE!!!"

Thank God for my catcher's mask,

because when the game started, I could hear the umpire dying from laughter behind me. Every time Puddin let out a squeal, he'd start in again. I couldn't wipe the crazy grin from my face, either.

Then, in the top of the third...The Coming. The Exodus. My own little league Apocalypse:

Puddin got loose on the field.

Bobbie had to "go shake the dew off her lily," so she'd put Puddin's leash under her chair before she went. Tommy threw yet another pitch in the dirt, and the ball bounced between my legs and straight toward the pig. Puddin was like a poodle on Ritalin, straining for the ball and screaming, "Wheeeeeeeeee!!"

As I ran toward the ball, while it seemed like the whole Eagles team ran around the bases, Puddin jerked loose, toppling the lawn chair. I reached the ball first, snatched it up just ahead of Puddin's snout, and turned to throw. I was too late. The Edwards players were just standing there in front of their bench, looking uncomfortable.

"SQUEEEEEEEEEE!!!" The chase was on. Puddin ran like lightning onto the field, and about a dozen players, parents, and coaches gave chase. Dr. Heigel (Sieg Heil!) led the pack as they scampered after her.

Freeze frame.

This is what's burned into my memory: I was 11, it was a gorgeous June afternoon, and a pig named Puddin was being chased around the bases by a Nazi psychiatrist.

Dr. Heigel (Sieg Heil!) finally caught Puddin and returned her to Bobbie, who scolded Puddin half-heartedly: "Awww, did a snookums get loooose?" "Squeek."

The game continued, but nobody much cared–they were all giddy from the parade of ham. The umpire kept right on giggling, and every few seconds he'd say to himself, "Unbelievable. Good God..." then peal off into more laughter.

Naturally, we lost 12-0. After the game, Puddin led the Lewises through the crowd to the tractor as if on a redneck red carpet. And if anyone asks me, I'll say without a doubt that yes, pigs *can* smile.

INTERLUDE:
Mississippi Educational Brilliance

When I was growing up, Mississippi was ranked 50th out of 50 in education in the U.S. And though I know the school systems have gotten infinitely better since then, I wanna share some book-learnin-type nuggets I experienced in school. (And sadly, every one of these is entirely true.)

For me—as for hundreds of my schoolmates, I'm sure—fourth grade was the Year of Punishment.

There was Miss Rothan, the math teacher. Though she taught multiplication and division extremely well, she had a temper. More often than not she'd throw chalk, an eraser, or whatever was handy, at a kid who gave a wrong answer.

Across the hall was Miss Rayburn, who taught reading and used an unusual method of punishment. Instead of taking you out to the hall for a whoopin, she'd say, "Commere, boy." Once you got to her desk she'd thump you on the forehead with her middle finger.

That finger was about the size of a magic marker, and the nail as big (and as thick) as a nickel, so along with the half-hour headache came a big red mark in the middle of your forehead that left you looking like a Pakistani immigrant.

At the end of the hall was our history

teacher, Miss Lee, otherwise known as Evil Incarnate. In addition to giving brutal paddlings on an almost daily basis, sometimes she'd make a kid come to the front of the room, tell everybody to put their heads down, then make the kid hold out his hand and give it a vicious smack on the palm with her paddle.

I gotta give her credit, though; she was creative. If a kid REALLY acted up, she'd make him do The Scarecrow. You'd have to stand at the front of the room holding an encyclopedia in each hand while your arms were extended parallel to the floor. After five minutes your bony little arms would be DONE. But if you even started lowering the books, she'd say, "Boy, GET them arms back up!"

So it's no wonder that, at the start of the year, the fifth grade teachers were always amazed at how well-behaved their new students were.

Sixth grade, though, was a walk in the park. We'd been warned by older students about Miss Thomas, the science teacher, who was in her 70s and suffered from mild dementia. Before she retired at the end of that school year, Miss Thomas tried to teach us that:

A. The sun has a bright side and a dark side.

B. We travel around the sun once every 24 hours, thus giving us night and day.

C. The moon is only a few miles from Earth.

D. All the lunar exploration is a hoax, and the lunar landings were filmed in Hollywood.

Fortunately, we were already old enough to know better.

Then there was my ninth grade Civics teacher, Miss Wilson. She clocked in at about six feet, 250 pounds, and had a big greasy red afro. She'd sit at her desk grading papers, alternately scratching her oily head with her pencil and chewing on the greasy end of it as she graded. (Was she thirsty? Or hungry? I could never figure it out.)

Anyway, she'd come around to each student to check our homework about twice a week. I sat behind Carol, who was smart as a whip and who, unlike me, always did her homework.

Carol and I had a system: Miss Wilson would check Carol's homework, and while she was writing down Carol's grade, Carol would hand me her homework over her other shoulder. I'd erase Carol's name and write mine, then Miss Wilson would check "my" homework.

So it's no wonder that to this day I know absolutely nothing about Civics.

5. A RAFT RACE IN PARADISE

(Soundtrack: GRATEFUL DEAD—"High Time")

It was the most beautiful place on Earth, but that didn't stop the gods of fate from having a ball.

There I was, 3,000 miles from home, an employee of that Hippie Valhalla, and I was winning the raft race. My partner Troy and I were paddling like mad as we made the last turn, the finish line only a football field away. We were gonna win! The raft behind us had no chance. It was over. In a few seconds, we'd be champions. Yes! We were gonna WI–

Except for that damned branch.

****

In the spring of my senior year of college, I realized I'd had enough. Six years of higher learning had taken their toll, and I was burning out fast–I had senioritis to the worst degree.

Then I heard about Yosemite.

I was dating some neo-hippie chick at the time, and it was all she talked about. She was a senior too, and was driving cross-country the day after graduation to work at Yosemite National Park, three hours due east of San Francisco. I knew very little about the park, and

I only knew the word because of the Looney Tunes character. "I'm the rootin-est, tootin-est, shootin-est..." You know the one.

I'd seen pictures of Yosemite Falls, but the moment I laid eyes on my girlfriend's photos of the park, I was in love. (With the park, not the girl.) El Capitán, Half Dome, the Fire Falls...it seemed like heaven compared to Mississippi, where the highest point of elevation was about 800 feet.

And though I really had no intention of getting serious with Neo-Hippie, the idea planted itself in my mind: Maybe I could work there, too.

I mean, Neo-Hippie got a job, and it had taken her two years to finish her final semester. So I researched it, weighed the pros and cons, and placed a call to the Yosemite employment office. About ten seconds into the conversation, my worries were over. It went something like this:

Me: Yes, I'm calling to find out information about seasonal employment, please.

Him: Oh, dude, you wanna work here, huh? Sweeeet. Lemme put you on hold for a sec, okay?

Me: No problem.

Him: All right. Peace, brother...

(The hold music was a Muzak version of the Grateful Dead's "Truckin.'")

Him: All right, dude, let me get your address and phone number, and we'll send you an application.

I gave him my info, then came this exchange:

Me: Just so you know, I'm graduating in May, and–

Him: Oh, sweet, man. We have lots of dudes who come here right after high school. So let me–

Me: No, college. I'm finishing *college* in May.

Him: Ooohh woooow. College!? Dude, I'd be sooo stoked to have you work here, man!!

Me: Ahhhhhh....okay.

And so, two weeks after graduating, I headed to California. Just before I bought a plane ticket, I'd found out that my friend Paul, whose brother worked at the park, was making the trip just a few days before I was to report there. Another buddy of his was tagging along, too, so after I'd packed most of my possessions in storage, the three of us loaded up Paul's Mustang and set out.

The trip was, as I'd expected, full of wonder and excitement. None of us had been anywhere west of Texas, so after we drove through Dallas, we were in uncharted territory. We had a firm plan: Chow down on Tex-Mex in Albuquerque, throw a penny into the Grand Canyon, then head north and play the slot machines in Vegas. From there it was just a hop, skip, and jump to the Sierra Nevada.

When we entered the park, my stomach roiling with excitement, the road went through a tree. Not around it, not under it, but right *through* the trunk of a giant Sequoia. I could scarcely believe my eyes, and I knew I was in for some adventure. Though we were actually in the national park, the valley—the populated part, the hub of activity—was still a few miles away. We were like fussy kids, asking each other, "When are we gonna get there!?"

We rounded a curve in the mountain road, and suddenly we *were* there. Boy, were we ever. Our first real sight of Yosemite Valley was like a punch in our collective stomachs, and our reverence knocked us into silence for a few seconds. "Oh...my...God..." Paul said eventually, echoing what we were all thinking.

We had an informal orientation, which included a tour of the employee campgrounds and an introduction to assorted personnel. My eyes stayed as round as saucers for a day or two, because everywhere I looked was like a postcard photo. I was bowled over by the beauty of the place, and I had a hard time wrapping my brain around the fact that I now actually lived there.

The employee grounds were...well, rustic. My cabin was about twelve feet square, made of canvas, with a filthy wooden floor. There was a communal kitchen/bathroom building, with individual lockers for food and cooking supplies. I had to hike about a hundred yards up the mountain if I wanted to crap, shower, or eat, but I didn't care (not at first; by the end of the summer, I learned that every single employee, me included, had pissed the bed at least once out of sheer laziness).

And the employees themselves? I can sum it up in two words: Hippie fucking Central. Name the cliche: patchouli, dreadlocks, bare feet...these folks had it. I'd say, oh, one of every ten females bothered to shave her legs and armpits. People would meet at the kitchen at 4:20 every single afternoon for...well, if you didn't already know, "420" is California police code for possession of marijuana. And baths? Fuhgeddaboudit.

My roommate, Troy, was a rare exception, thank God. He was from New Orleans, my neck of the woods, and was part Native American, part Hispanic, part...aw hell, Troy was a mutt. We spent countless nights drinking Sierra Nevada Ale and laughing at our dirty hippie co-workers.

Through some stroke of luck (or maybe because the personnel guy had been so stoked to have me work there), I ended up with probably the best job in the park, as a server in the fine-dining restaurant in the lobby of the Ahwanee Hotel, the five-star joint in the center of the valley. By summer's end, I'd waited on a variety of celebrities—and let me tell you, there's nothing like serving escargot to Carrot Top.

My first day at work, as I was being taken on the usual "get-acquainted" tour, I was repeatedly struck by an overwhelming sense of déjà vu: *Why the hell does this all seem so familiar?* I kept thinking. It was when I went into the dry-goods storage room that it hit me. "Potatoes, flour, croutons…" my manager was telling me, but his voice had morphed into Scatman Crothers's, and Scatman was saying, "Dried goods…canned goods…five whole chickens…eight gallons of chocolate ice cream…" *The Shining! This was the room that Nicholson was locked in!!!*

As if reading my mind, the manager suddenly said proudly, "You know, a lot of movies have been filmed here, too. Ever seen *The Shining?*"

I explained to him that yes, it was only one of my all-time favorites. And for the rest of the summer, I felt simultaneously frightened and proud every time I went in there.

About a month into my stay, I returned to my cabin from work one day, and the employee camp was deathly silent. None of the usual music was playing, no one was beating non-rhythmically on a drum.... *Something's up*, I thought. I saw Bill, the hippiest of all the hippies, sitting on a rock and staring into space.

"What's going on?" I asked as I walked over.

"He's gone, man," Bill said. "He's...he's in that great drum circle in the sky, man." A single tear rolled down his cheek.

"Who's gone?"

"Jerry, man! Jerry died. Bout two hours ago. It's...I just can't believe it." He started sobbing like a child.

"You...you mean lifeguard Jerry?" I said, referring to a fellow employee who worked at the pool. "How? Did he dr–"

"No, asshole, *Garcia*! Jerry Garcia died! OD'ed on smack. Only the greatest guitarist we've ever had, man!" Then he began singing: "We can have us...a high tiii-iiiime...Livin...the good liii-iiiife..." His song dissolved into moans of grief.

That was the first time I felt glad that my job was only seasonal.

The summer wore on, and I made new friends, learned to rock-climb, and did some hiking. And more hiking. And even more hiking. My favorite excursion was a three-day affair that took us into the deepest part of the park. While camping one night, we heard some evil, sub-human grunts and growls, and after some stealthy investigating, we saw three black bears feasting on a caribou they'd apparently caught.

About a month before my job ended, I was napping in my cabin when Troy burst in holding a yellow flyer. "Dude, we gotta do it!" he said breathlessly. The flyer advertised for the "Annual Employee Rafting Regatta," on the Merced River, a small waterway that ran through the valley.

"Dude, how can we lose?" Troy exclaimed. "Look who we'd be up against! These Granola-eatin assholes couldn't paddle their way out of a friggin bathtub." He was right, too. We'd been rafting a few times before, and the Dread-Head Crew, as we now called them, were about as athletic as Bill Gates with a heart condition.

"It's on then," I said.

****

The race began at 8 the next Saturday morning, and we were psyched. We did a couple of practice runs in the days leading up to it, and we had our route carefully planned out. There were maybe thirty of us competing, and as we jockeyed for position at the starting line, the combination of patchouli and body odor formed an almost visible cloud.

POW!! Hippie Bill had somehow found a starter's pistol, and we were off. Troy and I quickly broke into the lead, followed closely by lifeguard Jerry (not Garcia) and his girlfriend, Grace. But it wasn't a race, not really. Troy and I had a system: Five strokes on one side, then switch. If we needed to turn, Troy, who was in the rear, would call "Left!" or "Right!" to steer us in the appropriate direction.

And it was working even better than we'd hoped. At one point I glanced over my shoulder, and we'd left the others in the *dust*. We rounded the last curve and sprinted towards the finish line.

"Branch!! Right, right!" Troy shouted. Immediately I saw it: a tree limb, its sharp point barely submerged, was directly in our path.

When we hit it, Troy was thrown forward into me. *Psssssshhttt...* I knew what the sound meant: The raft had impaled itself on the stick. We began sinking quickly, but we weren't ready to give up.

"Go! GO!!" we both yelled, tripling our efforts to paddle, but within seconds the raft was overflowing with water.

I had a panicked idea. "The bank! Go to the bank!" We waded to shore, dragging the raft, which had become insanely heavy. Out of the corner of my eye I saw Jerry and Grace glide past us, bellowing with laughter.

We reached the bank, heaved the raft

out of the water, and turned it on its side to empty it. "Come on!" I yelled. We grabbed either side of the raft and began sprinting towards the finish line. Just as we were catching up to Jerry and Grace, Troy tripped over another branch and tumbled into the river. Not that it mattered by then; Jerry and Grace had already crossed the finish line. Half the crowd cheered, but they were all doubled over with laughter at our misfortune.

****

We were listed in the employee newsletter as finishing fourteenth out of fourteen. That night, we heard a knock on our cabin door, and there Jerry (not Garcia) waited with half his earnings from the race: An ice-cold twelve-pack of Sierra Nevada Ale.

"You deserve this, man," he told me. "Hell, you should have it all. You won the regatta today, man, no doubt."

"No we didn't. You did," I answered. "But you know what? I'll never forget that race. It'll make for a helluva story someday, too. So I'm glad it happened like it did."

"Me too," said Troy, and we raised our bottles in a toast.

I left Yosemite about three weeks later, on a bus that went from San Francisco to New Orleans in, oh, only about three days. (Because of our zig-zagging route, Texas took us a whole day to get through. A whole *day*!) My father drove down to pick me up, and on the way home, as I stared out at the passing pine forest, I realized I'd forgotten how flat Mississippi is. Flat or not, though, it was good to be home.

And since then, I've stuck to canoes.

INTERLUDE:
No Mo Sco!!

Playing high school football has given me some of the best memories of my life. I played all four years, and we were pretty damn good—we had an 8-3 record all four of those seasons.

Our coach, Coach Granberry, was REALLY good. In addition to knowing a lot about the game, Coach bore a pretty good resemblance to, and had the same icy stare as, NFL coach Jon Gruden.

I think my favorite thing happened my sophomore year. It was about midway through the season, and we were playing a team from Taylorsville. They had an incredible kick returner who'd already run back five kickoffs for TDs.

And against us, he ran two kicks back for TDs in the *first half*. I was on the kickoff team, and as a painfully slow white boy, I had no chance of catching him—much like most of the other players.

So of course, we kicked off to them to start the third quarter. Lined up next to me was a guy named Leroy Scott, and he was INCREDIBLY fast. In the huddle before the kickoff Leroy simply said, "No mo sco!!" As we lined up for the kick I could hear him muttering, "No mo sco... no mo sco..." under his breath.

So the guy received the kick, and of

course he broke into open field to score yet again. From where I was about 40 yards behind him, I remember Leroy chasing him....and it was like he hit a turbo booster. Leroy caught up with the guy in two seconds flat and tackled him at midfield.

I don't recall whether we won or lost that one...but to this day I use the phrase "No mo sco" every chance I get.

6. NO STEREO SOUND FOR ME (1988)

(Soundtrack: HARRY CONNICK, JR.—
"There Is Always One More Time")

I'm totally deaf in my right ear.

I wasn't born that way. Nor did my hearing loss gradually present itself, as it does many deaf people. It's because since I was a kid, I've been reckless. Ever since I can remember, I've acted before I thought. It's a fault that's cost me dearly.

Among other things, I've lost several jobs because of my carelessness. In one instance, I martyred myself by telling my boss what everyone else only thought: "You're a bitch, and everyone knows it." That was the end of that period of employment.

Another time, I kicked an extremely beautiful lady out of my house right in the middle of a hot make-out session. "I don't mean to be rude, but...you need to trim your nose hair," she told me as we paused to catch our breath.

"And *I* don't mean to be rude, but you should just get the hell out." It was the first thing that came to my mind; had it not been for my smartassed-ness, I probably would've gotten laid that night.

My recklessness has also almost cost me my life. I was mugged and beaten practically to death by a loser I met in a bar near closing time.

That ended my acting career, since I now have terrible vertigo when I stand, and when I talk, I sound like Mushmouth.

And I can only hear *in mono*. When I was eighteen, I felt invincible, and one night I had in mind what I thought was the greatest prank idea of all time. Little did I know that instead, the joke would be on me.

****

In June following my high school graduation, I was having the sort of fun most eighteen-year-olds have: getting drunk on cheap beer, playing summer league baseball, and practicing nonsense every chance I got. I think I felt the need to shout to the world, "Hey, look at me! I'm an adult! Look at what all I can get away with!"

There was a rather large community college that took up most of my town, and that summer I befriended some of the older students, since I planned on attending there in the fall. One was an almost mirror image of myself named Dylan, who became like a big brother. He was charming, popular, and funny, the sort of fellow I aspired to be.

Dylan worked as a lifeguard at the campus pool, and he lived in the brand-new dormitory at the edge of the college grounds. Along with several other buddies, Dylan and I spent many a night in his dorm room, playing quarters with Milwaukee's Best and celebrating our new manhood.

And every summer, the college hosted a two-week-long camp for high school students called Boy's State. The American Legion sponsored it, and one scholar from almost every high school in the state was invited to attend.

The boys at the camp stayed in the same dorm as Dylan, and for some reason, the counselors were militant about security. Everywhere the campers went, they were required to wear white T-shirts printed with "Boy's State." The counselors carried walkie-talkies, and they would stalk the dorm at night saying things like "State Boy Leader, the Rooster is in the Henhouse" into their radios.

One night, about halfway through a case of Schlitz tall-boys, I had my flash of inspiration. Dylan was working at the pool the campers used, so he had several of the T-shirts himself. Just as I was getting ready to bounce the quarter into the shot glass, I paused, staring into space.

"I've GOT it!!" I said. "You guys up for some fun?" Of course they were. The plan was this: we would all put on a T-shirt, then run out of the dorm, making the counselors think we were members of the camp. Never mind what would happen if we got caught; the thrill of the chase was all we could think about. And never mind that we were too drunk to give the counselors a run for their money—we couldn't consider anything except how much fun we were going to have.

About ten minutes later, the side door to the dorm burst open, and we all broke into the night, laughing. I heard behind me: "State Boy Leader, we've got squirters at Area One! I repeat, squirters at *Area One*!!" (Yes, squirters. I kid you not.) When I hazarded a glance over my shoulder, I saw several counselors chasing us. As I watched, a lean black counselor rounded the corner of the building like a shot, gaining on us like we were standing still. *Jeez, Carl Lewis has nothing on this guy*, I thought in my drunken panic.

As planned, at the corner of the adjacent building we split up, like a fighter squadron out of *Top Gun*. I broke right, and over my shoulder I saw the black counselor follow me. He said calmly into his radio, "Leader, I've got the skinny one. State Four is on the case." Because I'd played baseball practically since I was in the womb, I was plenty fast, but Carl Lewis was faster. When I looked again, he'd closed half the distance between us, gaining more ground every second.

As I tore around the corner and down the sidewalk, I saw a possible escape route. A darkened doorway, probably to a storage or electrical room, was coming up on my left. Before Carl Lewis could round the corner, I sprinted through the doorway....and into nothing.

****

The doorway led not to a utility room, but to a concrete stairway. Like Wile E. Coyote off a cliff, I shot off the landing, running on air for a few feet before I fell. I landed hard on the right side of my head on the bottom step.

As I lay there unconscious, another friend of ours, Joe, ran inside. Apparently, he either already knew what the room was, or he could see better than I could, because he didn't make the same mistake I did. He waited until the counselor chasing him ran by, then started to leave. He looked down towards the bottom of the stairway, and must have seen the dim outline of my prone body.

He told me later that he'd trotted down to me, thinking I'd either passed out or fallen asleep as I hid.

"John, c'mon, man," he whispered. "They're gone. John! C'mon, John, they're g–"

He froze when he saw the blood dripping out of my ear. Then, as Joe bolted up the steps and out the door, the pursuit eerily reversed itself.

"Hey!! Over here! There's a guy hurt!"

The chase was over.

****

The ambulance driver was a guy I'd been to school with who was also named John. He told me afterward that he and the other EMT's had strapped me in, my head directly behind John's seat. A couple of miles into our trip–the nearest hospital was about fifteen miles away–I woke up, moaned a few times, then sprayed vomit all over John and the rest of the cabin.

My memory of the ambulance ride is hazy, of course, but I recall how everything spun. The feeling was similar to the time I'd actually gotten inside a dryer at the laundromat and a friend had turned it on. I'd lasted only a few seconds, mainly because of the heat, and I'd vomited repeatedly after I'd spilled out onto the floor.

I spent the night in the emergency room, my sister Ginger dragging herself out of bed to stand watch over me (an experience that she would repeat under much worse circumstances about fifteen years later). The next morning, she guided me to the car and we went home, where I stayed on the couch for the next two weeks.

I had a tiny skull fracture as a result of the fall, and it had occurred in the inner workings of my right ear, which caused my auditory nerve to split in two. I went back to the hospital a couple of days later, where the doctor determined that I had absolutely no hearing in that ear. "It might be because of dried blood and fluid in the canal," he told me.

"We'll examine you again in a couple of weeks, and I bet by then you'll be just fine." *No, I won't,* I thought, but I agreed, smiling like the trooper I was.

My follow-up visit included a comprehensive hearing test, which I failed miserably. "If you hear anything at all in your right ear, raise your hand," the nurse said. I did raise my hand a few times, but only because the sound was so loud I actually *felt* the tiny headphone speakers vibrate. So that was it. I had officially become half-deaf.

The blow had shattered my cochlea, which controls balance, so for about two weeks, whenever I stood, everything spun like the dryer-ride. And for a few months, whenever I'd close my eyes and try to walk in a straight line, I'd walk in a 45-degree angle to my right.

The worst, though, was the ringing. You know how when you leave a concert, the music leaves your ears humming so that you talk really loudly? "HEY, THAT BEASTIE BOYS CONCERT WAS GREAT!" you yell. Well, it was like that, only times a hundred, with no actual sound to accompany it. I also had trouble determining which direction sounds came from. If someone behind me or on my right side called out to me, I'd turn to my left to answer them.

I've since adjusted pretty well. What makes the human body so great, I think, is its ability to adapt. I eventually walked in a straight line again, and the direction issue is long gone. The ringing is still there, but my brain has trained itself to ignore it most of the time.

I constantly hear people say with pride, "I don't regret anything I've ever done." Well, I do. I'm incredibly remorseful about all kinds of things.

Mouthing off to my bitchy boss. Kicking that gorgeous lady out of my house. Losing my fiancée. Almost dying. That list is so long, I could write another whole book on my regrets alone.

Even after all the mistakes I've made and the suffering I've endured because of it, there's one thing that gets me out of bed in the morning:

I'm alive.

I'm alive, and each day will get better. I'm built to be the most hopeful guy you'll ever know. Hope–the promise that tomorrow will be better than the day before–is our greatest human quality, I think. So what if my track record totally belies that idea? I don't care. I can't affect the past. I can, however, affect the future, and I wake up every day ready to tackle whatever the day will bring.

What is it they say? "What doesn't kill us makes us stronger"? I'm here to tell you, my friend: Hercules has got *nothing* on me.

INTERLUDE:
The Metallica Theory

Okay, here's something that's been rolling around my mind lately. Stay with me on this one.

Metallica should cover every song ever written.

The next time you're in the car, sing every tune like James Hetfield would. Tons of tunes take on a whole new life. "Morning Train" by Sheena Easton? Instant classic. "Medieval Woman" by ELO? Equally as good, especially if you echo the chorus. And the entire Elton John catalog instantly becomes genius.

My all-time favorite, though, has to be "Hotel California" by the Eagles. The phrasing, the rhyme scheme...the lyrics are just perfect. Next time you hear it, give it a try and go for some Metallica flavor–you'll see what I mean. Here's a sample:

"There she stood in the doorwaaay-ah

I heard the mission bell-ah

I was thinkin to myself this could be heaven or this could be heeelll-ah.....

Then she lit up a can-duuu-uuuhlll
and she showed me the waa-aaay-ah

There were voices down the corridoooor-ah

I thought I heard them saaaa-aaaaay-AH!"

Brilliance. Pure brilliance. There are exceptions, of course: No AC/DC of any kind. And no Foreigner, either, except for "Waiting for a Girl Like You." Otherwise, it's open season.

7. DIONYSUS PULLS THE STRINGS (1970)

(Soundtrack: MARY J. BLIGE—"No More Drama")

Even while I was still in my mother's womb, life was drama.

I know that sounds pretty self-indulgent, but I'm not kidding. From the moment I decided to enter this world, it seemed there was always one emotional episode or another surrounding my very existence. Whether it was just luck of the draw, or that God decided to save up a lot of His earthly conflict for me...that's neither here nor there. I'm just giving you the facts, ma'am.

And I'm starting to believe that instead of God, maybe Dionysus was the divine being that pulled on the puppet-strings of my life. Dionysus was the Greek god of drama, and he's obviously taken great pleasure in dealing me a deck full of conflict cards. (I'm surprised I don't have a birthmark in the shape of drama masks.)

And the spectacle all started the second I began my journey down my mother's birth canal.

****

It was a gorgeous April morning, and Mom was at home with my sisters, Liz and

Ginger, and her own Aunt Vera, when her water broke just as they were finishing breakfast. Mom had recently split up with my dad, so Mom and my sisters were living with my grandparents in their enormous, antebellum-style house. I mean, after a few minutes there one would expect a fat, Aunt Jemima-looking black lady to pop out and tell them that she didn't know nothin bout birthin no babies.

My grandparents had flown to Houston a couple of days before. Granddaddy had to have emergency heart surgery, and Houston was the nearest place for him to get the specialized operation he needed. Mom says that, if they couldn't find a friend or neighbor to take her, they had a plan: since Aunt Vera didn't drive, they would call a cab if Mom had to rush to the hospital, and Aunt Vera would stay home and watch my sisters, who were only two and three years old. It was a plan of last resort, I think, because in my hometown, not many people used taxis—especially not folks who lived three miles or so outside the city limits.

So no one was there to drive Mom to the hospital when she went into labor. (Isn't that more dramatic? Of course it is.) It was about 6:30 a.m., and apparently, the moment Mom had her first contraction, Liz and Ginger were arguing over who had gotten the biggest serving of eggs for breakfast. While Aunt Vera tended to my sisters, Mom called the cab company herself, breathlessly giving the dispatcher directions to the house. But for some odd reason—probably because she had a baby trying to exit her womb—she didn't tell him exactly what was going on, only that they "really needed to hurry." After she hung up, she, Aunt Vera, Liz and Ginger went out to the front porch to wait.

Well, they waited. And waited. Then waited some more. After about thirty minutes, just as Mom was about to pull her bottom lip over her head, Aunt Vera calmly said, "You know, maybe I'll call the cab company again. Maybe they can't find the house. Yeah, that's a good idea."

"YEAH, THAT MIGHT BE A GOOD IDEA!!!" Mom screamed between contractions. Aunt Vera sauntered into the kitchen as if to get another glass of iced tea. It turned out the cab in fact couldn't find the house, so Vera gave them directions again, casually mentioning that the passenger needed to go to the hospital because she was having a baby.

Apparently, the taxi company got the message, because a couple of minutes later, a cab screeched into the driveway (even though the driveway was made of gravel; I'll never know how a car's tires can squeal on rocks, but it happens on TV all the time). As Mom waddled out to get in, she noticed Aunt Vera walking beside her.

"Aunt Vera! What...are you...doing!?" Mom managed.

"Well, we're going to the hospital, aren't we? And we need to hurry! I bet you'll have that baby any minute now."

Have mercy.

"Aunt Vera!! You...need to...stay here...with the kids!!"

Vera paused for a moment, confused.

"Ooooohhh, you're right! Okay then. You go on." She turned and moseyed back to the porch.

When Mom opened the door of the taxi, a wave of body odor slammed into her nostrils. As she squeezed in, she uttered a quick prayer that they please, please make it to the emergency room—she couldn't bear the thought of this filthy cabbie putting his hands down there to deliver me.

She's since told me that, as they screeched back onto the road, she saw his hands in a death-grip on the steering wheel...and his fingernails were black from the grime underneath. "Oh, please hurry!" she cried.

"Goin as fast as I can, ma'am!" Dirty Fingernails said.

After running several stoplights and passing many cars on the right—something considered a mortal sin in Mississippi—they made it. As the taxi slid to a halt at the emergency room entrance, Mom could feel herself starting to streeetch—she couldn't hold me in much longer. The cabbie sprinted inside and came back seconds later with a nurse. It was 7:20 a.m.

****

"Jeez, honey, you're about to pop! Let's get you up to the maternity ward," the nurse said calmly.

"OKAY!!" Mom tried to sound equally calm but failed miserably. The nurse helped her out of the cab, saying, "Come on, honey, I'll help you. There's an elevator right inside."

"OOOOOH BOY!!" As they walked towards the elevator, Mom thought, *Hospital? Wheelchair? Does this damn place have one!!??* Apparently either they didn't or the nurse just thought she didn't need one.

They went into the elevator car, and Mom saw buttons for eight floors. And of course, just as Dionysus must have directed, the nurse pushed the top button. She then opened a small metal door beneath the buttons and pulled out a phone. Into the receiver, she said, "This is Nurse Anderson. I'm on the way up with a live one!" She hung up and slammed the little door shut.

The nurse smiled. "Maternity's on Eight. Hang on, honey!"

"GO TO HELL!" Mom answered like something out of *The Amityville Horror.*

They started up. And of course, Dionysus played another card. Seconds into the ride, the button for the fourth floor blinked on. About that time, Mom says, she felt something in her uterus give....and she knew it was about to happen. "OOOOOHHHH....." she yelled as fresh pain shot through her torso.

A bell dinged when they stopped on Four. The doors took about five minutes to open before another nurse scurried on. She looked at Mom, who was drenched in sweat and making whistling sounds.

"What's wrong with her?" the second nurse asked.

"She's about to—"

"OOOOOOOOHHHH!" Mom screamed.

"SHE'S ABOUT TO HAVE A BABY!!" The first nurse yelled to be heard over Mom's bellows.

"Oh. Congratulations," was all the second nurse said as she reached over and pushed the button for Seven.

Jesus Christ, another stop. "I DON'T THINK I CAN M—"

"You're doing fine, honey. Almost there." As the elevator continued its ascent, the nurses chatted about their plans for the weekend. When they arrived on Seven, the doors opened and the nurse exited. Then she turned, remembering something.

"Oh, I forgot. Bill says he has to—"

Mom pushed the "Close Door" button. "THANK YOU!!"

As the elevator rose one more floor, Mom says that, since this was her third child, she knew it was time. The feeling was not unlike trying to pass a bowling ball.

"OOOOH, HERE IT COMES!!" she screamed as the doors slid open. The nurse's frantic call must've worked, because there was an empty stretcher and a battalion of doctors waiting for them.

After that, Mom says, everything is a blur. She remembers being lifted on to the already-rolling stretcher, her feet being placed into the stirrups. "Fully dilated. I can see the crown," someone said. They rolled into another room, where Mom says she blacked out for a bit.

When she woke up, the first thing she saw was a doctor holding me while another cut the umbilical cord. It was 7:30.

"It's a boy! Congratulations, Miss Turner!" someone exclaimed. "Boy, that was a close one!"

As a nurse wiped me clean, Mom said, "My purse...where's my purse? I need to pay for my cab."

****

My grandparents returned home a couple of days later. They heard me crying as they hurried up the front walk. Inside, they held their grandson for the first time, and the first scene of the first act was finished.

INTERLUDE:
Closet Boy

My mom was a college psychology professor for almost 40 years. As part of her lecture on the stages of child development—including the Oral Stage, the Genital Stage, etc., if you follow Freudian psychology—she'd tell a story about an incident, I guess you might call it, that she had with me when I was about 2. (She first told me this when I was 12 or so.)

Apparently, she opened the closet door one day and saw me sitting there naked, just checking out my little package. So she did what any normal mother would do: she just closed the door to let me continue my business. (She used this as an example of a normal child's sexual development and exploration.)

And she kept telling the story to her classes as I got older. Cut to the summer after my tenth grade year, when I worked on the maintenance crew at the college. One of my co-workers was Mike, the quarterback of the college football team and all-around Big Man On Campus.

One day I told him my mom taught psychology. "Oh yeah? Who is she?" he asked me. When I told him her name, he said, "Cool. I had her as a teacher."

About five minutes later, he busted out laughing. "Wait a minute! That makes you the Closet Boy, right??" And the realization of what he meant hit me like a...well, like a sack of nuts, so to speak.

I was friends with a lot of Liz and Ginger's friends, many of whom attended college there already. So within days, I was no longer known as John.

"Hey, look! There goes Closet Boy!!" I must've heard about 30 times over the next few weeks. I made Mom PROMISE to stop telling that story to her classes—and though I'm sure she made good on it, "Closet Boy" was a name that stuck for a loooong time.

8. CONFESSIONS OF A GIMP (2002)

(previously published in
the October 2004 issue of *PulpLit*)

(Soundtrack: FOO FIGHTERS—
"Times Like These")

Gimp (gi'mp) *(Slang) n. 1. A limp or limping gait.
2. A person who walks with a limp.*

I'd always found this term hilarious, but
had really made it a part of my vocabulary since
I'd heard it in *Pulp Fiction*. My buddies and I,
kind-hearted as we tried to be, always had an
inner group-guffaw whenever we saw someone
with a physical ailment. "Indeed..." one of us
would say, our unspoken like-mindedness like
some weird version of menstrual
synchronization.

Already wobbling through life as a semi-
successful actor, I was modestly surviving a
Gen-X lifestyle, and had recently moved to
upstate New York from my home in the Deep
South to begin a new contract. For us starving
artist types, it was a darn fine job. My new town
was a burg of about 30,000 tucked into the
Finger Lakes region. I was a New Yorker after
being there about an hour. The lakeside
community oddly resembled the Civil War-era
river town of my roots, and seemed to be a
comfortable, crime-free nest.

Surrounded by similarly jaded types over a long period of time, I'd developed an attitude of detached cynicism about my existence–any Steely Dan fan will understand. I reacted to every social situation like that guy at parties who ridicules people behind their backs (and come on, you know you love that guy!) Prime example: my co-workers and I would occupy ourselves during the maddening hours on the road by coming up with names of recipes that contain the meat of retarded people. "Mongoloid Mutton!" someone would yell with glee. "Ground Down's!"

In our desperate abandon, we would've made a great case-study for Maslow's Hierarchy of Needs. You remember Maslow, right? His theories are based on a pyramid of life needs, with food/shelter/nurturing at the base; a person's needs become more complex as the pyramid goes up. Our "need" for entertainment is probably in the top .0005 percentile, so you get my meaning.

My lack of awareness of the challenges that lay ahead for me is filled with a certain self-empathy–how on Earth can one prepare for something like this? One can't. Believers in karma could have a field day; I smile to myself even now when I think about my ignorant bliss of years ago.

****

I remember strange, vivid dreams about being a guest at different people's houses, and hoping they didn't think it strange that I kept wanting to take a nap. The weirdest one was of an Englishman who kept a spinning wheel next to the couch I was sleeping on; I also kept trying unsuccessfully to light his pipe on a wood-burning stove.

Ginger, God bless her, played James Taylor's "Greatest Hits" nonstop on a CD player by my bedside for pretty much the entire time I was in a coma. I'm sure that music helped keep me alive. (And even now, when I hear one of those songs, I just…go somewhere else for a moment.)

My memory of events during what doctors refer to as an "open-eyed" or "vegetative" coma is hazy at best. I'm told now that upon my emergence from the coma I was a complete jerk, mean to everybody. I think my body was shutting down all auxiliary power–it was too busy keeping me alive to worry about stuff like what was for breakfast.

I turned into the quintessential problem patient—biting nurses, refusing to see visitors, yelling at Liz for folding my clothes, even telling doctors that their breath stank. "This behavior is normal," they said. I think it was all part of reaffirming my foothold in consciousness. To quote Gloria Estefan, I was coming out of the dark.

****

That day a month before had played out pretty ordinarily, starting with my reluctant attendance to the first day of yet another dead-end, part-time job. *I'm starving for my art, dad-gummit!* I would tell myself. I'd always had an overly rosy outlook on life, sometimes to a fault; I always believed my big acting break was just around the next corner. So on I slaved, unaware of how profoundly my life was about to change.

The day wore on as most others, ending with yet another evening of that public baring of souls we call "clubbing." I consider myself strangely but thankfully fortunate that the entire night has been erased from my memory, as a result of either the ungodly amount of alcohol I consumed, or just a simple gift from God; from what I've pieced together from police reports and eyewitness accounts, I was "politely asked to leave" after being "overly friendly" to some of the female patrons around closing time at a nameless bar. It was there that I met Natsu; he and I supposedly ate at a nearby diner shortly thereafter, with yours truly paying the entire tab.

CUT TO:

EXT. NIGHT-CITY STREET

JOHN

(Slurring drunkenly) Dude...you
know what would make this night
purr-fect? A big fat joint,
man...

NATSU

Aw, man, that ain't no
problem...you bought my food n'
stuff...C'mon—in here...
(They step into an alleyway, and
moving into some shadows, start
smoking a joint that NATSU has
produced.)

EXT. NIGHT-ALLEYWAY

(They talk and smoke for a while;
JOHN, becoming increasingly
incoherent, falls silent.
Suddenly, NATSU punches JOHN
hard, knocking him over. NATSU
kicks at his face, JOHN
instinctively covering himself in
the fetal position. After a few
more kicks, NATSU takes JOHN's
wallet from his back pocket;
rifling through its contents, he
pockets the cash as he runs away.
JOHN lies motionless behind some
overturned garbage cans.)

An old woman who was leaving her
apartment building the next morning honked

twice at me. When I didn't move, she got out, annoyed. 'Another drunk,' she thought. A few seconds later, she was running to the door of the adjacent laundromat, her mind in a panic after seeing my bloody face and bruised body. I was rushed to the hospital, barely alive. Later that day, after I had been identified by my boss and my mom was flying cross-country in terror, I was transferred to a better-equipped facility in the neighboring metropolitan area. Six months of terrible re-birth followed.

****

Traumatic Brain Injury (TBI) *(Phrase) n. Damage to brain tissue caused by an external mechanical force, as evidenced by loss of consciousness due to brain trauma.*

My overeducated guess is that my injury was to the cerebellum and/or brain stem, which form the control center of the brain and therefore the entire body. The damage is mainly to the centers for balance and fine motor movement, but I think the brain is such a complex "machine" that damage to any part of it lessens its effectiveness as a whole.

I can now barely walk, and when I do the process is mechanical, almost as if my brain were following some Twelve-Step mantra, taking it "one [step] at a time." That's how I walk–step by step. The whole procedure could be considered normal, except I resemble a slow, jerky version of Pinocchio.

I once described to a therapist this constant condition of vertigo: You know that state you're in just before you fall back in your chair, after you've leaned back just a liiiiitle too far? That momentary feeling of "OH-AAAH"? That's the best thing I can think of for comparison–now imagine feeling that way every time you stand up.

My speech–one of my strong points as an actor–is now like listening to a person talk with a balled-up sock in his mouth. (The irony here is strong enough to stand on its own, I know.)

My stepfather and I still joke about one of the customers at his gas station, an ancient, kindly wisp of a man named Mr. Martin. He would walk in slow, small steps, sometimes taking five minutes to get from his car to the station office. To be funny, Sonny and I would do the "Martin Shuffle" in the parking lot of a restaurant or other public place. Needless to say, I am now the Martin Shuffle *master*! Hierarchy of Needs, again, I'm sure.

I think the biggest blow to my lifestyle is that now it takes for-EVER to accomplish small tasks. The process of getting ready (or doing the three S's–Sh*t, Shave & Shower) used to take about 30 minutes, quick bite included. It's now maybe twice that; sometimes I forget, and run late–a vice I previously despised. In a nutshell, I'm "forced" to slow down; the upside is that I never have to be in a hurry. (Hey, I'll play that cripple card every chance I get.)

I sometimes swallow incorrectly, with food or drink going down my windpipe instead of to my stomach. I yawn incessantly when tired, but when I attempt sleep I lie awake watching the History channel or infomercials, hoping they'll bore me into slumber. I win small victories when I rediscover a forgotten pleasure, such as walking to the corner store; major projects like dancing are out of the question. Welcome to my world.

****

Sympathy(sim'-puh- the) n. *1. A feeling or expression of pity or sorrow for the distress of another. 2. Compassion or commiseration.*

My six-month hospital stay is full of anecdotes both amusing and heart-breaking. Among others, there are always those characters who gravitate towards anguish, as if they need it to remind themselves they're doing OK. I told one of these "repeat" visitors never to come back because her patchouli was scaring me.

There was the Singing Nurse, who would warble show-tunes, a musical Florence Nightingale who did a daily dance with death through the ICU. Then there was my neurologist, who would pinch my cheek with all his might to wake me up; he'd yell in his thick Middle-Eastern accent, "JUHN!! JUHN!!

WAKE UP, JUHN!!" One day a guy in a nearby bed answered, "No...I don' wanna." Oh, I got a million of em!

As if in some hideous joke, time strode firmly on. Tears were shed, promises were made and forgotten, holidays were celebrated, jobs were gained and lost. My first words after emerging from the coma were "Harlem Nights." Seems Ginger was watching it on TV, and asked someone else in the room what it was, so I answered her–she said afterwards that she nearly jumped out of her skin.

I recovered at a snail's pace, making infinitesimal but constant improvements. The milestones, simple as they were, seemed huge: feeding myself, standing up, going to the bathroom on my own...new projects came, were conquered, then instantly taken for granted again. "Oh, you're doing so well!" I heard again and again from people with reassuring grins plastered to their faces. I still don't know whether I believed them or thought it was just false encouragement.

Since my attack had happened in a small town, the legal proceedings came and went in a blur. Most of the folks involved must have believed in a "fair and speedy trial," because only about a month passed between my first interviews with the D.A. and the sentencing. Natsu was a repeat offender, so the judge happily, sternly doomed him to 25 years with no possibility of parole. Gotta love those

Neighborhood Politics...

To add irony to the headline-making case—remember, this was a small town–Natsu's father is a well-known, well-respected local reverend. Not farcical enough? All right, here's more: jammed right into the center of town is a federal pen, famous for its harsh treatment of inmates.

The biggest advance was my transfer to a rehab facility, where I crashed for 3½ months. Nestled in the suburban hills, my new unit was the site of innumerable "rebirths"; the whole place gave off a good vibe. I was finally able to take stock in my unbelievable new life; my adventures at the other hospital still seem dreamlike. I became much closer to my family, who was always there to chase away the boogey-man named Death. My siblings and parents alternated taking the sad, 1,300-mile flight to my bedside so that I would never be alone. My mom, knowing I'd always been a huge Harry Connick, Jr. fan, actually emailed him. What she expected him to do, I don't know–the whole situation stank of a bad movie of the week.

****

Four roommates (and what seemed like twelve lifetimes) later, I was sprung. My last (and lengthiest) roommate was a tragedy of a man who could no longer walk or speak, but was otherwise healthy. Timothy would have long conversations with his wife, but all he could really say is–let me see if I can spell it right: "Ge-PAT-te-pa-te-pa-te PA PAAA!" It was heartbreaking to listen to; the inflections and emotions remained, but Timothy's words were just unintelligible. Before my eyes, he dissolved into a sad, broken picture of frustration, and cried himself to sleep most nights. I felt I had *become* Maslow by that point.

Home I went, overwhelmed by my new lease on life. Twenty of my former co-workers descended upon my empty, sterile apartment; like a ten-year-old with a new pet, they had me moved in and set up in a half-hour. To underscore the bizarre social situation, one guy showed up just as they were finishing, and proclaimed much too loudly, "Hey! I thought we were gonna have pizza!" Words to live by.

****

So here I sit some 15-odd months post-beating, trying to eke out a living in my new but still seemingly fruitless profession. "Oh, you're doing so well!" people say, but this time there seems to be an air of sadness behind their pasted-on grins. I toss off names of my "new writing projects" like so much fluff, trying (mostly triumphantly) to remain the cool, brooding-but-successful artist type. When Meredith Willson wrote "The Sadder But Wiser

Girl" for *The Music Man*, he probably had no idea how universally dead-on it was.

"So why write about it?" you're probably asking. The truth is, I'm really not sure. All I know is that it feels good to be sitting here at my computer, finally rid of these particular monsters. I guess a synopsis of my experiences will allow me to both escape from and embrace the whole blessed thing.

I think I need to make a disclaimer, too, however reluctant it is: I am not perfect, nor do I ever claim to have been. I'm selfish, forgetful, greedy, vain...but whose list wouldn't be endless? (At this point I could say that I, with all the life-blows I've taken, have every reason to be cynical; truth is, I was cynical before this happened.)

I can sum it all up with a saying I heard from some barfly years ago—a quote that I've held on to: "Life is just too screwed up to be taken seriously." My God, truer words were never spoken.

To add the final piece to this puzzle—the perfect tutorial on irony—I just started yet another part-time job as a "greeter" at a very well-known department store. The feeling of coming full-circle is amusing and overwhelming; the only difference now is that everyone's kid gloves are just too big.

It's a perfect opportunity to give ol' Maslow's theories a gut-check: My favorite customers are those wanna-be old ladies with their fake furs and too much anti-wrinkle cream, who rush into the store as if they actually have more pressing matters to tend to; the demand is usually something like, "Can you put that wide-screen in the *back* seat?" I always look at my walker, then back at them, and say through the balled-up sock, "No, I can't. But I'll be glad to find someone who can..." One lady actually shed a tear after she realized.

And that's what keeps me hangin on–the fact that, no matter what happens, I can always find a way to laugh.

INTERLUDE:
Stupid Assumptions

I went to Burger King today, and as I was approaching the door, some lady was standing there holding it with the all-too-familiar "you're crippled, so you must be an idiot too, so I'm gonna be EXTRA nice to you" shit-eating grin on her face. And by now, you know I fucking hate that shit.

I got an idea, just in case she kept up her patronizing ways, and sure enough, she didn't disappoint. "There ya go, buddy...good job!" she chirped as I shuffled through the doorway. *Hey lady, YOU asked for it.* "Thanks." I leaned in close and whispered, "Hey, just so you know...I'm about to rob this place."

She just stared at me. "You...you what?"

"I'm gonna ROB this place!" I gave her a maniacal grin, unzipping the bag I was carrying. "Here, I've got a gun—"

"OH!" She scurried over to a man—probably her husband—sitting at a nearby table. "Let's go. C'mon!" She sounded desperate and scared, which almost made me bust out laughing. "Hey, I was just kidding," I called to them as they quickly left through the rear entrance. I just shrugged and went to the counter to order.

OK, I know I'm an asshole...but it just goes to show you that if you make stupid assumptions, you might get more than you bargained for. "Good job," indeed.

9. THE MIDGET BOX TURTLE (1980-82)

(Soundtrack: JOE COCKER—"You Can
Leave Your Hat On")

Thanks to my two older sisters, I spent an inordinately large part of my childhood naked.

Now, I dearly love me some Elizabeth and Ginger. One is a science teacher and mother to three outstanding boys, and the other is an administrator at the community college in our hometown.

My parents divorced when I was less than a year old, and Ginger and Liz are two and three years older than me, so until my mom remarried when I was 13 I was the only male in the house, and the youngest.

(Looking back, and knowing the roles family circumstances can play, it's really a wonder I'm not a huge queen. Somehow I dodged the gay blade.)

Anyway, from the time I was 10 until she married Sonny, Mom taught a night class at the community college, leaving us at home alone for hours at a time. "I really felt like your sisters were old enough to take care of you," Mom said later. "When I think about it now....hmmmm."

And overall, Liz and Ginger took great care of me, what with the cooking dinner, making sure I had my bath and helping me with my homework. But they also used the unsupervised opportunity to wreak some childhood havoc.

I think those baths started it all. The girls struck first one night as I came out of the bathroom, my 10-year-old body dripping wet and clad in nothing but a towel. When I came out they jumped me, ripped off the towel, picked me up (even dripping wet, I weighed *maybe* 80 pounds) and carried me, screaming, to our front door.

Like an epileptic tabby cat, I was trying to slither out of their grasp while I hollered...but they had me good. They threw me out the door into the empty carport, then turned on the carport light.

I was bawling and screaming, "LET ME IN LET ME IIINNN!!!" while I pounded on the door, but apparently they thought that wasn't attracting enough attention. So the girls flung open the living-room window and started yelling, "Heeeyyyy!! Hey, look over here!"

We lived in the faculty housing neighborhood across the street from the college, part of which was a circle, with the furthest of the 20-odd houses maybe 80 yards away.

So as I beat on the door, out of the corner of my eye I noticed numerous carport lights coming on. About 40 feet away, the front door to our next-door neighbors' house opened, and Mrs. Simon poked her head out.

"Hey, is everything all r—OH!!" She

slammed her door shut after seeing my tiny, lily-white behind.

And did I mention it was about 30 degrees outside? I was soaking wet and freezing, and...well, you know what happens to a guy's nether regions when it's really cold. (My 10-year-old midget box turtle had crawled inside its shell, is what I'm saying.)

After a couple of minutes they still hadn't opened the door, so I took matters into my own little hands. I retrieved a length of rusty pipe from the utility room, went around to the back of the house, and shattered Liz and Ginger's window with one mighty swing. I broke out the remaining glass and dove inside.

When Mom got home I ran to her car (fully clothed now, thank you) and told her what had happened. I expected her to flip out, but she just looked tired and sad.

"Guess I'll put some extra blankets on the girls' beds," she said.

I don't remember exactly what their punishment was, but I do remember it was severe, and they didn't get their allowance for like the next three months because of the window (even though *I* was the one who had broken it).

The next summer, they took advantage of my naivete' once again. I was—and still am—a very trusting soul; I guess I assume, sometimes to a fault, that people will just do the right thing.

Well, in this particular instance my sisters did nothing of the sort. We took a vacation to Houston, and one night the three of us went swimming in the hotel pool.

The pool was in the atrium of a three-story Holiday Inn, so we took the elevator down from our third-floor room and walked around the building. Bonus! We had the pool to ourselves.

After a game of Marco Polo, I was flopping around in the deep end when the girls excitedly called me over.

"Hey! Wanna do something fun?" Elizabeth asked.

I should've smelled trouble right then, but of course my innocent mind just wanted to please. "Sure!" I said as I hung onto the ladder.

"Okay, here's what we'll do: We'll each give you a dollar if you take off your swimsuit and swim to the other side and back."

In retrospect, I have no *idea* why I didn't catch on, but I was just glad they were paying attention to me. "Cool! I'll do it." I was mentally picturing the gumball machine in the hotel lobby, which I would raid with my hard-earned...booty, so to speak.

So, taking a quick look around to make sure we were still alone, I peeled off my suit with one hand while I clung to the ladder with the other. "Here, hold this." I handed them the suit.

(Don't say it. I know.)

"Go!!" they both said, and I pushed off the wall and swam like a turtle (a midget box turtle, of course) to the other side about 15 feet away. And of course, when I got there and turned around...

The girls were sprinting toward the door to the parking lot, cackling maniacally. "Ha ha ha.....BRAT!!!" I heard Ginger yell as they went.

So there I was.

The pool area was silent except for the gentle lapping of the water. I hung on to the ladder and started sobbing. Now, I was thin, having played baseball since I was 6, and I was swift as the wind. My midget box turtle and I psyched ourselves up for an insane dash back to the room.

I think it was about 80 yards from the pool to the elevator, and my lily-white behind covered that distance in about, oh, two seconds. I was lucky that, since it was about 10 o'clock on a weeknight, I didn't encounter any people during my sprint.

I got to the elevator and pushed the Up button, then tried to hide next to a fire extinguisher on the wall.

When the door opened, I held my naked breath as I hugged the wall next to the door. After a second or two, no one came out, so I peeked my head around. *Whew!* Empty. I scurried inside, pushing "3" about ten times.

Suddenly I heard the door to the parking lot open, and loud men's voices. *CLOOOOSE, door!!* I thought as I started sobbing again. The doors slid shut…but just before they closed a hand came snaking between them. They opened again.

Several men in business suits entered the car. They didn't see me at first because I'd tried to squeeze my body all the way into a corner. "Hey, I've heard she'll su–Oh! look here!" one said. The men all stared when they saw me, making me cry even harder.

"What's goin on, boy?" another asked as I sat curled up in the corner. Through my tears I told them what had happened, and after all the laughter died down, one of them got me a towel from the front desk.

Apparently Mom already knew all about it, because when I got back to the room she was watching TV while Liz and Ginger sat on their bed, looking guilty and smug at the same time.

"Girls?" Mom prompted them, never taking her eyes from the screen.

"We're so-oorryyy," they chorused, Ginger mouthing the word "brat" at the end.

So it's no wonder I chose acting as a profession. I'd spent so much time showing my ass, both literally and figuratively, I figured I might as well get paid for it.

INTERLUDE:
Don't TOUCH the F*cking Fruity Pebbles!!

One of the gifts Ginger gave me for Christmas recently was a box of Fruity Pebbles. When I unwrapped it, I was confused, until the memory socked me upside the head, so to speak.

When we were in high school—I was a freshman when Ginger and Liz were in 11th and 12th grades, respectively—I was, well, a jackass. We all loved Fruity Pebbles, and after a while I got in the habit of practically pouring the whole box down my throat when Mom got home from the grocery every Saturday, just so the girls couldn't have any.

So Mom started buying one box for me, and one for them. I usually ate mine within maybe a 36-hour period...and at first I'd leave the other box alone.

That changed one rainy Monday morning. I went into the kitchen before school to eat breakfast, knowing I was myself Pebble-less. Jackass that I was, I got out their box, poured myself a heaping helping and started munching away.

Well, Liz wasn't having it. When she walked in and saw me eating Pebbles, she asked me if that was from their box. "So what if it is?" I said. "What're YOU gonna do?"

POW!!! Liz rared back and DECKED me. I toppled over in my chair as blood squirted out of my nose. Liz grabbed the cereal box and told me there was more where that came from, if I kept eating their Pebbles.

Hey, I KNOW I deserved it. And to this day, every time I eat a bowl of Fruity Pebbles I get a runny nose.

10. THE ONE ABOUT THE CHRISTMAS TREE (2005)

(Soundtrack: TRADITIONAL—"O Christmas Tree")

The Grinch? Bah Humbug. Ashes and switches? C'mon, guy. I friggin *crushed* my parents' tree, on Christmas Eve. You like that? That's just how I get down. That's how to celebrate the birth of *Christ*, my friend.

It was the old Trip Home to Meet the Parents deal. Stephanie, my fiancée, had never flown before, and she suffered from bad motion sickness, so we had the Dramamine and the barf bags ready when we boarded the plane. When we took off, I expected Uncle Ralphie to show up, but Steph was a perfect trooper–she told me later that it had been no problem at all. The one time we did hit turbulence, she turned pale and closed her eyes, but she rode it out, and no chunks were blown.

In the airport, I was nervous, though I had no reason to be; Steph was an angel, and my folks loved her from the moment they met. So home we went, oblivious to the insanity that awaited us.

My folks are....*particular* about how they do things. They just prefer things as they like them, regardless of whether or not it makes sense to anyone else. Their quirks and bizarre habits have made them even more endearing to me, and I thank God every day that I grew up surrounded by wackiness.

And the thing that always makes Christmas special at my parents' house is their tree. Early each December, Mom walks in the woods until she finds just the right one–a cedar the right shape, the right height, and all the rest. Except that her idea of the perfect tree is one about four feet tall, with maybe four or five ornament-worthy branches. (A Charlie Brown tree, in other words.)

One year I asked Mom why she got one like that, expecting to hear that she just picked the first one she came to.

"Oh, noooo. I look all over the woods to find just the right one," she corrected me. "Since the house burned we don't have a lot to decorate with...and honestly, Sonny doesn't like them to touch the ceiling. I don't know why. The best thing is, cleaning it up's a snap. Once you get everything off, you just break it apart and put it in a Hefty bag, and you're done."

Little did I know how funny that statement would later be.

As expected, Stephanie laughed when she saw it. (And how could she not?) She was to sleep in the guest room, and even though there were two beds in there, I slept downstairs in the living room. I wanted to be respectful, as any good son should be. (Actually...as we were walking through the airport Mom had said, "I've got the couch all made up for you." Her accompanying look told me not to argue.)

So, late that Christmas Eve, after the annual phone conversations with relatives and a long Christmas snuggle with Steph, I headed down to the living room. I stopped in the kitchen for a drink of water, unplugged the Christmas lights, and went to sleep on the couch.

Which was right next to the Christmas tree.

That water I'd drunk is what started it all. Sometime during the night, my bladder filled up–as bladders tend to do–and I went to go pee.

Since part of my brain damage affects my balance, it takes two or three seconds for the room to stop spinning when I stand up; the vertigo is worst when the room is dark, and the living room was pitch-black. When I rose to my feet....

Whoah-oh-WHOOOAAAAAHH! CRASH!!!

My full weight fell directly onto the tree. I felt ornaments explode, presents crunch on the floor, and the trunk snap like a toothpick. The branches scratched my entire body—I had on only boxers—and a small twig pierced the skin on my back. I rolled off and slowly stood, brushing off the cedar and taking inventory: *Head's okay, my back's cut open, I can feel it bleeding, arms, legs...* I was just fine. Other than the blood dripping from the gouge in my back, I was all right.

So...now what? In the darkness, I could barely make out the outline of the dead tree. I did the only thing I could: I left it. (I had the crazy belief that hey, no one'll notice.) I scurried to the bathroom and put a bandage on my back, even though it had already stopped bleeding, then crept back to the couch and hid under the covers till Christmas morning.

****

"Merry Christmas, everyb–" When I opened my eyes, Mom was standing at the bottom of the stairs, staring at the flattened tree.

"What…what happened?" She looked like she was trying to figure out who'd run over the dog.

"Aaahhh….I, ah…fell down."

"Last night?"

"Yeah. I got up to pee and lost my balance." Mom was silent as she walked slowly to the pile of cedar. The gifts sat underneath it, forgotten.

"Well…are you okay?"

"Oh, I'm fine." She lifted up what remained of the tree. The gifts seemed okay too, except for one big box that was as flat as a pancake.

"Hm." I wasn't going to hazard a guess at what that meant.

The door to Sonny's room was on the other side of the tree, and now it opened.

Sonny took a step or two, but the tree blocked him from going further.

"Damn." He moved the tree over and walked around it. "John Boy, we don't *fall* on the Christmas tree in the middle of the *night*." I love when he jokes like that.

"You mean you heard me!?"

"How could I not have? I was sound asleep, and boom! Down ya went, boy. I thought about comin to check on ya...but if you was hurt, you'd holler, and if you was dead, you'd keep till mornin." Somehow, Sonny always keeps things in perspective.

When Stephanie came down a little later, she had a big laugh. And she howled when she looked at the couch—it was all but covered with cedar.

We opened our gifts, Sonny playing Santa by pulling the presents from underneath the tree. As it turned out, the gift I'd flattened was only a sweater, which Sonny had wrapped in a huge box to fool Mom.

As we ate the traditional Christmas brunch, the dead tree lay exactly where I'd fallen on it. That afternoon, when the extended family came, everybody had a good guffaw, but the tree stayed right where it was.

The next morning as Steph and I flew back home, that tree found its final resting place in a Hefty bag at the bottom of a gully. There it has surely begun to turn into a fossil, but for one shining moment, that tree was the center of my wacky universe.

INTERLUDE:
Holy Sh*t—Literally!

OK, this one gives "Praise God, from whom all blessings flow" an entirely new meaning.

One year when I worked for the newspaper in Auburn, I covered a Christmas play at one of the churches. The last scene was a living Nativity, complete with live animals— one of which was a donkey whose name was listed in the program as Burrito.

And if you're unaware, the formula for animals onstage is, "Live animals + human audience = massive amounts of feces."

The formula played true on this December night. Here's how it went down: a cast member led Burrito onstage in the last scene. From Burrito's position in the tableau, his backside faced right where I was sitting.

After a couple of minutes, the donkey's handler slowly placed her hand on his butt, where it stayed for a good twenty seconds. *Why...why is that lady fondling a donkey's...well, ass?* I thought.

Then she took her hand away, and I understood. Burrito let loose with a veritable chocolate waterfall. Not to steal focus from the show, the handler fetched a broom and dustpan and loudly swept up the, ummm....yeah.

The smell was ridiculous. The old lady sitting next to me just couldn't handle it, so after a few seconds of covering her nose, she got up and left. (To puke, I hope. Oh *please* let her have puked.)

The kicker is, the handler had been trying, literally, to *hold the shit in*. But Burrito was gonna have his time in the limelight, by God.

Literally. BY God.

(And I know you're probably thinking I got way more perverse satisfaction out of this than a mature human being should. But I don't care.)

11. PIGS IN THE YARD! (1987)

(Soundtrack: GREEN JELLY—"Three Little Pigs")

The poor pigs never stood a chance.

That afternoon, those unfortunate swine picked the wrong time, the wrong backyard...and, most definitely, the wrong flower-bed.

It was one of those lazy Saturdays that happen every once in a while. Sonny was gone for the afternoon, my mom was in the backyard watering the elephant ears, and I was snoozing on the living room couch, watching golf on the TV. (And you know why golf announcers talk so softly–they're afraid they'll wake you up.)

I was living the country-boy high life then, my teenage years thus far marked by few rules, many friends, and a car for my sixteenth birthday. I was quarterback of the football team, voted Class Favorite by my smallish junior class, and all-around guy-to-have-several-kids-by-the-time-he's-30.

I think it was then that whatever forces control my "bizarro" universe decided they were bored.

Our neighbors across the road, the Taylors, had a pen in their backyard where they kept several dozen pigs. It was maybe a half-acre of dry, grassless earth that absolutely reeked of pig poop on hotter days. I pitied the

Taylors for putting up with that god-awful smell just for a few extra ham-hocks with Sunday's stew.

Maybe two or three times in the few years we'd lived there, I'd seen one of the Taylors muttering to himself as he chased around a pig who'd somehow squeezed under the ramshackle fence. "Dammit, you bastard, COMMERE! Little...piece o'.....here! Soo-WEEEEEE!! Dammit....I'm goan..." As you can imagine, I always laughed to myself watching it.

But this time...well, this time was different. Not one or two, but *three* of the porky bastards had escaped. And they'd crossed the road, gone around our house, and were rooting away in my mother's carefully planted backwoods garden. I had just drifted off when the commotion started.

"PIIIIGGGS!!! Pigs in the yard!" Mom's scream startled me so much I fell off the couch. I jumped up and ran to the back window, where I saw the beasts getting *after* it, their snouts buried in the flowers surrounding the swing.

Just then the back door tore open, and Mom went past me in an almighty blur. (And damn, was she fast! She must've crossed the 80 yards or so of our backyard in about three seconds.) She went into her bedroom closet—what was she doing in there?—and tore back into the dining room carrying Sonny's 12-gauge pump shotgun.

Oh, Lord.

In one superhuman movement, she went through the door to our back deck and set herself in a shooter's stance. The pigs were still rooting contentedly.

BOOM!!! BOOM BOOM!!!

I think the first shot took out two of them, but then came two more shots for good measure. The post-blast stillness was eerie, except for the occasional scrape of one of the pigs' hooves as they kicked the ground. The swine all thrashed around as they died (and they were indeed dead; Sonny kept the shotgun loaded with buckshot, and the lead nearly split those pigs in two).

Mom lowered the gun and walked back inside. (And maybe my memory is playing tricks on me…but I swear she swaggered more than usual.)

"Hm," she grunted as she walked past me into her room.

I just stood there, dumbfounded. Should I call the Taylors? The police? Maybe fire up the grill? I was at a loss. I just shrugged and went back to the couch.

When Sonny got home, I ran to the garage and told him the story. Instead of laughing, or reprimanding Mom, he, too, just shrugged, as if this happened all the time. "Guess I'll call Stan to come haul em away." (Stan was Liz's boyfriend.)

So that night, beneath a couple of

makeshift floodlights, Stan and I loaded the dead pigs into the trunk of his '81 Nova, lowering the back end almost to the ground. Those pigs reeked of blood, shit, and death, and only added to the stench of the dumpster down the road that we put them in.

Yet out of it all came a memory I will forever cherish: a mental snapshot of my mother in her shooter's stance on the back deck, murdering the Three Little Pigs.

INTERLUDE:
The Mud Mobile

When I was in high school, my stepdad Sonny owned a full-service gas station right on the town square. One of his side businesses was buying used cars, fixing them up and selling them for a profit.

So every few months, I'd come home from school to find some old hooptie in our driveway. He always asked my sisters and me to test-drive them for a couple of days before he re-sold them.

And I think Sonny had a sense of humor when he was car-shopping: In the space of about two years, I got to tool around in an immaculate '73 Cadillac Brougham that was about 45 feet long, a mid-70s station wagon complete with faux wood side panels, and a '79 AMC Pacer, the interior of which smelled like cigarettes and ass.

But his genius purchase was a '74 Volkswagen Bug that was painted camouflage. It had 18-inch mud tires on the back and no rear fenders. It had fog lights on top, and in place of an inside dome light, there was a big orange siren.

Needless to say, we kept that one for a few months. And after a while, Sunday night became Mud Boggin Night. Since its engine was in the back, the car got unbelievable traction with the mud tires—it could go through mud that none of the 4x4-owning good ol' boys in town would dare attempt.

And because it had no rear fenders, that car would get COMPLETELY covered in mud. The deal was that if I went mud-bogging, I'd drive to school the next day so I could wash it after football practice.

I'd dig a hole in the mud on the windshield so I could see for the ten-minute drive to school. And driving that Mud Mobile through town for all to see, I'd literally laugh out loud.

12. THE FRANKIE JEAN LEWIS TRIP
(2006)

(Soundtrack: JERRY LEE LEWIS—"Middle Age Crazy")

I still sometimes think this whole thing must have been a dream. It certainly feels that way.

On a recent trip home for Christmas, Sonny took us to Ferriday, Louisiana, where he'd been born and raised. We went because Sonny had heard about a Jerry Lee Lewis Museum there, and since he's a cousin of Jerry's (he thinks), he was eager to go.

And hoo boy, did we *ever* go. We got oh-so-much more than we bargained for...from Frankie Jean Lewis, sister to The Killer himself. And not because she was sibling to a celebrity—oh, quite the opposite.

In fact, not two minutes after we met her, this happened:

As she was handing a six-pack of beer to the driver of a car in the drive-thru liquor store attached to her house (which also served as the museum), she said, "Damn. This town's 97 percent black, and five percent white...and hell, I don't know what happened to the other one percent." The car's two passengers, who were both black, didn't say anything.

I knew then I was in for a treat.

****

Growing up, I'd listened to Sonny tell countless stories about Jerry Lee. Though he said they were just "briar-patch kin," and I don't think they were actually close, I loved hearing Sonny reminisce about sneaking into the honky-tonks to hear Jerry play.

Shortly after I arrived home for Christmas, Sonny told me about the museum; within seconds we made plans to go. Ferriday is a town of a few thousand people north of Baton Rouge, just a few miles up Route 65 from Sonny's birthplace, which is a wide place in the road called Waterproof.

After a huge catfish dinner in Natchez, we crossed the Mississippi into Ferriday. As we entered the city limits, Sonny was bittersweet about the town's development: "None of this was here twenty years ago," he said. "This was all flat land, all the way to the river." The look on his face, though, told me he was remembering plenty of good times too.

Finding the museum was pure hell. After getting directions from some locals, we went up and down several side streets before stumbling upon a barn-like structure called "Lewis' Quick Drive-Thru." A tiny sign down in a corner next to the entrance read, "Home of the famous L wis Family Museum." (The "e" was missing.)

Driving into the barn, we saw shelves of liquor bottles and reach-in coolers full of beer.

"Damn. A drive-thru liquor store,"

Sonny said from behind the wheel. "I tell ya...they just do things different round here."

Different indeed. After we had waited for five minutes, no one came out to serve us, so we drove on through. Just past the exit was a large concrete slab leading to the door of a dilapidated house. Sonny pulled over, and we parked and got out. We just stood by the car, wondering what to do next.

After a few seconds, the door to the house opened, and a plain-looking woman with dirty, curly mouse-brown hair and thick glasses popped her head out.

"Hey-there-I'll-be-right-with-y'all," she said, and slammed the door shut.

Hmmmmmm.......okay.

We stood there confused until she came out again, introducing herself as Frankie Jean Lewis Terrell.

"I'm Jerry Lee's younger sister, and I– HEY!! Don't be ridin that damn bike through here!"

We turned and saw a young black girl on a bicycle at the end of the driveway, looking nonplussed.

"Hell, they always ride through here, blockin my damn driveway," Frankie Jean half-whispered to us. "And hey!! Dontcha be talkin to none of them boys up the street!" she yelled to the girl, motioning to a group of young men just up the block.

"Aw, them boys be my cousins," the girl

said.

"Yeah, one of em's prolly your daddy too," Frankie Jean whispered in our direction. "Damn darkies." She walked over to wait on the black couple who'd just pulled in.

Holy shit, is this really happening?? I thought as she held forth about the ethnicity of Ferriday's population. Her use of math had me puzzled too: *97 percent...plus five percent...plus one percent...that's 103 percent. Wow. I guess they add numbers differently around here too.*

After the couple drove away looking disgusted–they were, I assumed, used to Frankie Jean's behavior–she invited us inside the house/museum.

"All the museum stuff's this way," she said as she led us through a small kitchen. She stopped beside the coffee pot and held up a liter-size Crown Royal bottle filled with what appeared to be water.

"I swear this ain't liquor," she chuckled nervously. "I've just found that this makes me the perfect amount of coffee."

"Hey, that's...that's a great idea!" Mom said desperately. (What else could she say?) Frankie Jean took us into the den, which had a huge dining table, a bar, and an old upright piano.

"So this is it...the piano Jerry learned to play on." And I have to admit, it was kind of a magic moment, despite the bizarre circumstances. I felt kind of reverent standing next to the place where one of my heroes had spent hours learning to create his own kind of magic.

The moment ended instantly when a door opened and in hobbled Frankie Jean's daughter, who was missing a leg.

"This here's my daughter Marian. Honey, these nice folks are the Kellys, say hello." Marian just gave a small wave.

"Marian's gonna be gettin a new prosthesis pretty soon! Ain't you, sugar?" Frankie Jean said as Marian wobbled down the steps into the den.

"Hm," was all Marian said as she limped past us behind her walker, escaping into the kitchen.

"Y'all come on, there's more stuff in the living room," Frankie Jean said as she climbed the stairs. As we followed her, I stopped on the landing to snap a quick photo of the old upright with my digital camera. Frankie Jean was ahead of us, talking non-stop.

"Damn. Marian ain't got but two cigarettes left, and here she is done lit em both!" She gestured to an ashtray that held two Marlboros burning toward their filters. "Now that's what I call smokin!!"

I felt like pinching myself to make sure I was really awake.

The living room held another piano, a baby grand draped with a thick black covering, and a second dining table. On the table was a two-foot-tall bronze sculpture of The Killer pounding on a piano engulfed in flames. I whipped out my camera and snapped a photo.

"Hey sugar, I'll tell ya when you can take pictures, okay?" Frankie Jean snapped.

"Oh, yes ma'am, yes ma'am," I said, trying with all my might not to burst out laughing as I shoved the camera back into my coat pocket.

Every inch of the room's walls was covered with photos, articles, and other memorabilia. One whole side was dominated by his twenty-odd albums, all signed by Jerry himself.

"But ya know, it's the weirdest thing. Jerry ain't been here in bout twenty years," Frankie Jean said at one point. "Sure would be nice if he'd drop by for a visit." *I don't know about that*, I thought. *Put those two in a room together, and their combined redneck-ism might cause some kind of rip in the space-time continuum or something.*

My favorite thing, though, was in the hall. Jerry served a brief stint at a local seminary studying to be a preacher—"He was fired from there cause they caught him playin boogie-woogie in the church late at night," Frankie Jean explained–and some of his handwritten Bible lessons were taped to the wall. Wondering whether it was possible to be "fired" from school, I looked at the barely legible writings.

I didn't get far. "No. one: I no sining is

bad," read the first line of the first one. I had to step back into the living room to get hold of myself. Having seen most of the museum, the others followed me.

"So this here's the house," Frankie Jean said. "My folks courted and married here. Jerry Lee got married six times here." She leaned in close and said, "There've been four suicides here too. A couple friends, and two of my brother-in-laws.

"But hey, that's part of bein a Lewis. We just tell it like it is."

"Yes," Mom finally managed. We said our goodbyes, barely making it out the front door before we all erupted with laughter. Thinking our adventure was over, we got in the car and exited by the rear of the house.

Against the back wall stood a pile of broken liquor bottles, about eight feet across, and tall enough to partially obstruct the view from the kitchen window. We did the only thing we could do, which was howl with more laughter.

But there was one more priceless item. As we pulled onto the street on the other side of the house, lined neatly in the front yard were four small gravestones, marking real graves. Though the inscriptions on them were too small to read, my mind flashed back: *"Four suicides...."*

We were still giggling when we crossed the Mississippi River half an hour later.

****

I didn't dream that. It really happened. Sonny told me recently that he's going back soon, and he's taking his daughters from his first marriage, Lisa and Sandra, with him. "They need to be exposed to this woman, boy," Sonny said with glee.

Dream or not, I feel supremely lucky to have been treated to her mere presence. In fact, I think everyone needs a little Frankie Jean Lewis in their lives. Maybe they would start tellin it like it is, too.

INTERLUDE:
Nigras

When I was a kid, my grandmother was a dominant force in my life. She lived with my grandfather, until he died when I was 10, in a huge antebellum-style house just south of town. She had strict and proper values, and was the very epitome of a Southern Belle.

She had a slow, melodious Southern drawl, and...one of the words she mispronounced was her term for black people. She was saying "negroes," but it came out as "nigras." So to my young, uninformed ears, it sounded like she was saying "niggers."

I'd always wondered privately why she would call people niggers, until one afternoon when I was about 12, I heard my grandmother say, "Went to the grocery this morning......some nice nigra boy helped me with my bag."

"Mom, why does she call black people 'niggers'?" I asked on the way home. She looked confused for a second, then she howled with laughter.

After Mom's giggles subsided, she told me the way things were. And just like that, all those school beatings I'd received suddenly made perfect sense.

13. LUCI-FUR (1980-2002)

(Soundtrack: PINK FLOYD—"The Dogs of War")

Let me tell you about the animal Anti-Christ.

Now I love me some pets, don't get me wrong. All my life, there's usually been a dog or cat in the house. And when they have lots of charm and personality, they're better than a human roommate.

But for some reason, I've always been at the center of one creature catastrophe or another. Whether it's just my place in the universe, or there's some weird destiny lined up...that's not for me to know. I just believe that I was *built* to cause grief to the pet population.

And it seems as if there's been some higher force at work. Over the years, I've developed a theory that in some other plane of existence, some unknown dimension, there's a demon—a pet puppet-master, if you will—that controls the relationships I've had with the animals I've owned. I've dubbed this spirit Luci-Fur, and It has been grooming me for this terrible position since I was a lad.

It all started when I was 10. One of my chores then was to mow the yard on Saturdays. Our lot was pretty small–I could knock it out in about two hours–so it wasn't the most strenuous of tasks. One Saturday morning, after a bowl of Kaboom and some "SuperFriends," I went out to the utility room to get the mower.

Our cat Patches had just had kittens and they were still in her bed, which was a few feet away from the push-mower. (And yes, this is going where you think it is.) Their eyes were still closed, so they were milling about mewling when I came in. Patches jumped right onto her bed—maternal instinct—as I kneeled down to pet her. I gave the kittens some love, then stood up and dragged the mower to the door. I failed to notice that there was one kitten missing.

I rolled the mower into the front yard. Humming the Go-Gos' "We Got the Beat," I yanked on the starter rope. The mower turned over a couple of times, but it made a weird thunking sound. I pulled again. THUNK THUNK THUNK.

It sounded like something was caught in the blade.

Puzzled, I turned the mower over. What I saw made me sink to the ground in horror.

A black and white kitten had crawled onto the blade. Suffice it to say...it was indeed dead.

We buried the kitten in the yard that afternoon under a huge oak tree. I found a big rock to use for a headstone. And I cried myself to sleep for the next three nights.

Needless to say, I've been scarred ever since. And my involvement in pet tragedies has followed me like a shadow: A year or so after the mower incident, we got a dog from the pound. Arf, his name was (and I won't even go into my family's complete lack of originality when it came to naming pets). He was a Benji look-alike, and smart as a whip, but he loved to chase the other neighborhood animals. My afternoons were soon spent running up and down our street. "Arf! Here, you little...leave Miss White's ferret alo—ARF!!" It was ridiculous.

One morning the school bus was late. Mom was loading us into the car to drive us when the bus sped around the curve by our house, its horn blaring. As we started down the walk to get on, I saw Arf chasing a dog through the empty lot across the street.

My memory of this is all in slo-mo: The bus slows as it reaches our driveway. Arf chases the other dog across the street. The bus door opens, just as the lead dog exits from under the bus. My sisters and I begin screaming as the bus grinds to a halt...with Arf pinned beneath the rear wheel.

We howled in unison as the huge wheel spat Arf out behind the bus. I was light-headed, clutching at Ginger for support. From behind us my mom said, "Go on. Just get on and go!" As I climbed the stairs, I looked at Billy, our college-age bus driver. He was bawling. The last thing I saw before my house disappeared from view was my mom bent over Arf with a garbage bag.

That afternoon we buried Arf next to the kitten under the oak. Fortunately, Stephen King's "Pet Sematary" wouldn't be released for another few years, so my imagination was spared any late-night terror. From that moment on, it was as if Luci-Fur had branded me as one of Its terrible disciples.

During my junior year of high school, Luci-Fur struck again. A couple of years before, we'd moved to a house in the country. It was situated mere feet from a rural highway, smack-dab in the middle of a straightaway about a mile long. Cars would rocket by at 60 and 70 miles an hour, and going to the mailbox across the road was like playing a live version of Frogger.

One steamy May afternoon, Mom, Ginger and I were doing some yard-work out front. We had a pit bull-spaniel mix then, and his name was Dog. (I know, I know.) Dog was mean as a viper, and had attacked quite a few people–the meter-reader, a couple of family friends, even me. He loved Mom with a passion, though, and was crazy when it came to protecting her.

As we were picking up sticks in the yard (a chore that always bugged the hell out of me—WHY!? There's gonna be a yardful again in a week), Dog was prancing around, as always never more than a few feet from Mom. The mail truck had just pulled up to our box across the street when Luci-Fur tugged on his puppet strings.

Dog took off like a shot, fur bristling, towards the truck. Just as he was crossing the road, a car blew past, striking Dog head-on as it went by. It flew on down the road, the driver either too cowardly or too coldhearted to stop or even slow down. There was a brief silence, then we all began screaming. "Noooooo!!" Mom yelled, and we all ran to Dog. By then the mailman had gotten out of his truck to see if he could help. I ran into the house to get a sheet or towel for Dog.

We rushed him to the vet, but it was too late. The car had snapped his spine, broken both hips, and given him severe head trauma. That night, Mom held Dog's head as the vet slid the needle into his hip. The next day, we started another Pet Sematary, burying Dog right next to the garden.

We've since had several other dogs, but even now, over 25 years later, Mom says that none will mean as much to her as Dog did. And I can still hear Luci-Fur laughing.

I hoped that was the last of the disasters, but of course Luci-Fur saw that it wasn't. Fast-forward to my college years, when I was living with a couple of friends in a house right off-campus. A friend who was graduating gave us a cat–a little black-and-white beauty we dubbed Mr. Fatty, even though she was a female (and I'll admit, that was the weed talking)–who quickly became family. The neighborhood we lived in was pretty bohemian, sort of a redneck

Haight-Ashbury, and there were always stray cats skulking about.

Within weeks, Mr. Fatty was pregnant. An enormous tom everyone called O'Brien had pinned her down in the backyard…and that was all she wrote. As the time neared for her to give birth, I was told by a neighbor, who had four cats of her own, that Mr. Fatty's delivery might be difficult due to her young age and small size, and that I should watch her closely during her labor "in case you need to, ahhh...help out."

Help out!? Oh, Christ. Damn you, Luci-Fur!

And of course, it was worse than I could've imagined. When Mr. Fatty went into labor, her yowling and growling was like the voice of Luci-Fur Itself. Like Jorge Posada, I squatted down next to her bed to monitor the activity, cursing Luci-Fur the whole time. After about an hour, she still hadn't given birth to the first one, and I could tell she was getting tired. The kitten was being delivered breech, and with every contraction, a tiny tail and foot inched out, only to slide back in.

You might need to help out. So, summoning all my courage, I did. Every time the kitten appeared, I tugged ever-so-gently on the tail to try and coax it the rest of the way. I tried it a few times—nothing doing. So on the next contraction, I squeezed my eyes shut and jerked. I felt something give way, like pulling on a cooked spaghetti noodle until it snaps. I inched one eye open to see what had happened.

All I held was the tail. It had broken off in my hand.

"AAAAAAAAAHHH!!!" I screamed to the empty house. Not knowing what else to do, I threw the tail out of the open window a few feet away. On the next contraction, the kitten squirted into the world. Mr. Fatty had six in all, the rest sliding out easily.

Mr. Fatty, the bobtail, and the rest of the litter were all fine. In fact, the tailless one was the only one we kept. And to commemorate a poor sap who'd recently made headlines, we named him Bobbitt.

After that, I figured Luci-Fur was done with me. (Jesus, hadn't I had enough!?) No, It must've thought, I hadn't. A few years later, Luci-Fur was at it again. I'd moved half a country away to work for a children's theatre troupe, and my job afforded me a nice one-bedroom apartment. But I was a little lonely, so I decided to get a cat to keep me company.

My injury when I was 18 had made me completely deaf in one ear. Lo and behold, a friend told me he'd heard about a cat at the pound that had been horribly abused and was now missing most of one ear. Perfect! I figured that between the two of us, my new pet and I would have one complete set of ears. By the end of the week, she was snuggled safely in her new bed at my apartment. I christened her Van Gogh.

Unbeknownst to me, though, her

mangled ear was horribly infected. The following Monday, I left Van Gogh alone for the first time when I went to work. When I came home, my entire living room, including my off-white couch, was covered with droplets of blood. Van Gogh had been scratching her ear raw, and she would repeatedly shake her head, as if to physically shock her auditory nerve into working again. When she did–I witnessed it countless times–the blood would fly onto *everything*. I spent night after night with a bucket of hot water and bleach, scrubbing until my arm hurt. And every second I spent cleaning, I could hear Luci-Fur's evil guffaw in the back of my mind.

I took Van Gogh to the vet, where they cleaned her ear and gave me some ear-drops to stop the infection. That night, when I put the drops in for the first time, her cries of anguish once again had me thinking: *That's not her voice....it's Luci-Fur. And that's his way of laughing.* Alas, the drops didn't help. So Van Gogh kept bleeding, and I kept cleaning. And cursing.

A month or so later, Luci-Fur stepped aside...and the *real* Devil, ol' Beelzebub himself, went to work. I was mugged and assaulted, ultimately spending seven months in the hospital. Only after I came home did I get the full story about Van Gogh.

For the first couple of weeks after the attack, I was touch-and-go. My friends and co-workers kept an around-the-clock vigil in the

ICU waiting room, and I was told it was about ten days before someone thought to check on my apartment. One of my best friends, Jennifer, finally went there, and she's since told me that the scene was heartbreaking. Van Gogh had nearly starved to death, and the infection in her ear had spread to most of her body. Jennifer had no choice but to have Van Gogh put down. It seemed that Luci-Fur had finally declared himself the winner.

Since then, I've avoided having a pet at all costs. I've thought of getting a snake–I mean, how could I harm a damn *snake*!? (Then I realize that maybe it's not me harming *it* that I should worry about.) What drives me batty now is trying to figure out why. WHY, for Luci-Fur's sake!? Was I chosen at random, or has it all been a series of deadly coincidences? Maybe I'll never know.

In the meantime...my collection of stuffed animals has become enormous.

INTERLUDE:
Practical Joke for Dudes

In keeping with the mischievous spirit of Halloween, here's something fun for two guys to do (sorry, ladies!) next time you're at a bar/club/restaurant. It takes some special circumstances, and you wanna make sure the guy you pull the prank on doesn't know either of you—you'll see why.

Here's how it works: One of you goes into the men's room and stands at a urinal. Then the guy you don't know goes in—and it's guaranteed he'll give you a one-urinal buffer zone, as he doesn't want to be thought of as a perv. Then the other one of you goes in and stands at the urinal next to the first person.

After a few seconds, you (or your friend) will look over at the other one and say very casually, "Hey, nice dick."

"Thanks a lot!" the other one will respond cheerfully.

Guaran-TEED the third unknown guy will finish his bidness and be out instantaneously. It's fun!!! I've done it a couple of times—hilarious both times.

14. THE BROWN TWO-BY-FOUR (1990)

(Soundtrack: BEN FOLDS FIVE—"Regrets")

It's the regret of all regrets. The one thing I never, ever should've done. You know how people often say, "Oh, if I could only go back in time..."? It's that...to the thousandth degree. I'll admit, I've made plenty of mistakes in my life, but none of them quite compares to this.

I'll warn you, too...this is crude. I don't tell this story to be vulgar or disgusting on purpose, but to recount it exactly as it happened. So I'll get the nastiness out of the way right up front:

I made my girlfriend shit herself.

****

It was my sophomore year of college, and I was editor of the campus newspaper, a member of the Student Senate, and the announcer for the marching band's halftime shows. I was also active in the school's drama department, winning roles in almost every production. I had my fingers in lots of pies, so to speak, so there weren't many folks around campus who didn't know who I was.

One of the fringe benefits of my popularity was that I had a date almost every weekend. In a way, it was sad, because my dates became more like quests for another notch in my belt. If faced with the choice between a floozy or a wholesome girl, I'd pick whomever I could score with the easiest.

That all changed when I met Katy.

She was new in town, playing the lead role of Sandy in that semester's production of *Grease.* I was working backstage, and she and I hit it off from the moment we met. She was a beautiful redhead, a bit shy...but underneath her innocent exterior, I could tell a wildcat lay in wait.

We went to dinner on our first date, and I was in love from the moment the appetizers arrived. Our conversation flowed like water, and by the time the dessert came, it seemed we'd known each other for years. But I noticed that Katy only sipped at her glass of wine, finishing maybe half of it during the course of the meal. I dismissed it as an effort to keep control of herself, but my hormones wanted to pour the glass down her throat to, well, to ease her up a bit. I stayed cool, though, and suggested that we stop off at a local tavern for a nightcap.

"Well...maybe just one," she said. That was fine with me.

She surprised me at the bar by ordering a club soda. *Hmmm...this is gonna be tougher than I thought,* my hormones said.

Be careful! This one's marriage material... answered the shred of morals I had left. I decided to investigate a little.

"So...I'm curious. Why the club soda?"

"Well, I'm kind of embarrassed about this, but...alcohol does weird things to me. For some reason, one drink for me is like five or six. So I really have to be careful."

Bingo! "Well, don't worry. I'll never ask you to drink a drop," I answered like a gentleman.

"That's good to know. You don't want to see me drunk. It's...well, it's not pretty."

"Say no more." But my superego was screaming, *Do it, man! Get her plastered! She'll be putty in your hands!* But somehow, I silenced those inner voices and took her home. In the car, we kissed passionately, but some light petting was as far as I got. As I walked her to the door, though, I was already planning my next move.

Well, for the next six weeks or so, I was forced to keep it in my pants. Not that I really minded, though; I was head over heels for her. And every time we went to a bar, she kept the club soda industry in business.

All that changed on our next date. Boy, did it ever.

Grease had just closed to good reviews, and everywhere we went, people would say, "Hey, it's Sandy!" To celebrate, we doubled with two other cast members for Ladies' Night at a nearby club. Try as I might to remain the perfect gentleman, I knew I'd jump at any chance I got.

As we walked towards the club entrance, Katy said, "Hey, I might need you to take care of me tonight."

"What do you mean?"

"Well....I haven't really let my hair down with you yet, and maybe it's time I did." She gave me a sly grin. "So if I have a few drinks, promise me you won't let me make a fool of myself. Just....just take care of me, John." Her face was inches from mine.

Oh, baby, will I ever take care of you. "Katy, you don't need to say another word. You have a good time. I'll carry you to the car if I have to." *And lay you in the back seat, then drive to some deserted field, and....*

"No," I blurted aloud, telling my hormones to keep their cool.

"What?"

"Oh...nothing. What Katy wants, Katy gets, is what I meant to say."

And what Katy wanted...was me. When we got to the dance floor, Katy was only halfway through her first beer, but she started grinding. Can we say *Dirty Dancing*? She would've made Patrick Swayze blush. I was drinking water, making sure I stayed in control. I didn't want to be too drunk to, ahhh...drive, yeah, that's it. Too drunk to *drive*. I gulped the rest of my water, hot as a firecracker.

"Oh, Katy...wow!" I managed.

"Sweetie, you ain't seen nothin yet," she slurred into my ear. If my ear could've smelled her breath, it would've choked on the salty-sweet aroma of booze.

As the night wore on, I realized that when Katy told me alcohol made her lose control, she was putting it lightly. *Super*-lightly. After her second beer, we went out to dance again, and I had to hold her up to keep her from falling on her face. Even so, like the dutiful boyfriend I was, I made sure her mug was never empty. Looking back, I regret that more than anything.

After a couple more drinks...she was *done*. She spent the rest of the night in the bathroom puking, and I actually did carry her to the car. By that point, testosterone was guiding my every move.

She protested, though, when I tried to put her in the back seat. "Hey...whaddya doin?"

Damn! "I'm putting you in the back seat. Don't you want to lie down?"

"No....the fron'...I'll lie down in the fron'..." She waved a hand at the front passenger door. I hoisted her into the seat, trying to recall just how far back it went, and how much leg-room there was in case...in case...

Katy suddenly leaned out and puked on my shoes. I jumped out of the way, and she barfed several more times.

"I'm shorry, shweetie," she said as I wiped my shoes with a piece of paper I'd found on the ground.

"Hey, that's no problem. I've been there, done that." *Now what? She might pass out...and John, you know you're not into necrophilia. Damn!* Frustrated, I went around to the driver's side and got in, and we drove off.

That's when it happened.

After a few miles, as she reclined in the passenger's seat, she started moaning. I gazed at her. Even though she was shit-faced, and had just puked on my shoes, she was still as gorgeous as could be. I think my hormones were making a flank attack on my psyche, because her moans aroused me yet again.

"Bathroom...I need a bathroom..." she muttered. Having just shampooed my car's carpet that week, I didn't want any fresh puke-stains.

"Hang on. We'll be there in two minutes," I told her, my testosterone army retreating for the time being. There was a convenience store a couple of blocks ahead, and I pulled around to the back. Fortunately, the restroom doors were accessible from the outside; the last thing I wanted to do was carry her through the store and make the clerk think I was dumping a dead body.

I helped her to the door, and she said, "No I got it. I got it from here." She stumbled in, almost falling down.

"Okay, I'll be in the car. Just let me know if you...need a hand," I said as the door swung shut. *Please, God, please don't let her need a hand.*

As I waited, my morals and my hormones had a final, bloody clash.

Maybe she'll puke herself sober.

But not too sober! If she does, you know what that means. The only nookie you'll get tonight is from ol' Fistina.

Then Fistina it is! Haven't you heard of a little thing called "respect"??

Yes I have. But like the song says...I need to take care, T-C-B!!

I finally decided to be a good boy. Good things come to those who wait, and all that. Speaking of waiting...about ten minutes had passed, and no sign of Katy. Had she passed out? Died? What the hell was going on in there? Against my better judgment, I decided I'd go check on her.

When I opened the door...I got the surprise of my life.

She had, in fact, passed out. She was lying on her side on the tile floor next to the puke-covered commode, her back facing the door. Through the open stall door, I could see her prone body. Her pants and underwear were bunched around her ankles...and a huge turd was protruding most of the way out of her ass.

Oh...my...God.

I just stood there, flabbergasted. *What do I do? Wake her up? Go back to the car and wait? Look for a hose?* I figured I'd try to get her out of there before anyone else came along and witnessed what I'd just seen. I went to her, stepping over the brown two-by-four snaking its way along the tile.

"Katy. Katy, wake up." I shook her by the shoulder. "Katy, wake u–"

Her eyes opened, and in a millisecond, she was sober. She surveyed the scene as if she hadn't drunk a drop.

"Get the hell out!"

"But–"

"GET OUT!!" She didn't have to ask twice. I scrambled back to the car. A couple of minutes later, she came out, looking like...well, looking like her boyfriend had just seen her shit herself.

As she got in, I tried to console her.

"Katy, I–"

"Shut up."

I didn't argue. How could I?

The ride home was silent, except for my fits of giggling when I would mentally replay what had just happened. When we got to her house, she got out and slammed the door without a word.

****

I broke up with her the next day, as much as I hated to. I just couldn't handle it. Every time I recalled the image of her beautiful face, it was instantly replaced by one of her lying on the floor with a huge stink-log sticking out of her butt.

Even now, two decades later, I tell the story to anyone who'll listen. Matter of fact, a couple of years ago a buddy told me about a theory: If I tell enough people, it might actually get back around *to* her, without the person telling the story knowing that it was her that did it. Can't you just picture it? "Hey, let me tell you this great story I heard about some chick who shit herself..." Oh, I hope.

Is that wrong? Without question, it's wrong. Katy was too sweet to deserve such a fate. But in the meantime...I hope my new girlfriends drink club soda, too.

INTERLUDE:
Women's Poll: Do You Hover or Cover?

One day a lady in the office next to mine popped her head in our door and said that the women's restroom on our floor was out of order—the toilet was broken—and to either use the men's, or the ladies' on the first floor. My co-worker, who's incredibly female, said there was no WAY she was using the men's.

That prompted an earnest 10-minute discussion of what ladies do when they don't want to sit on a nasty-ass pee-covered seat. She told me about two distinct methods:

"Hovering" is when a lady drops her drawers, hangs her junk over the bowl and hopes she has good aim. (This is my co-worker's preferred method—but she said it takes a good eye, otherwise she'll do like us dudes and cover the seat).

"Covering," obviously, is when you put TP all over the seat, then take care of bidness like normal.

I'm thinking of conducting a telephone poll on the matter, so if I call your house asking about your peeing habits, don't think I'm a pervert.

15. THE LEGITIMATE TERM PAPER EXCUSE (1988)

(Soundtrack: RUSH—"Tom Sawyer")

I think I'm one of the few people in the history of high school with a truly logical reason for not turning in my term paper. It wasn't because I didn't finish it, or because I lost it, or that I was sick that day. Hell, my dog didn't even eat it.

It was because, when the paper reached approximately 300 degrees Fahrenheit, heat decomposed some of the cellulose material, causing it to ignite. This produced smoke, made up of hydrogen, carbon and oxygen. The compound molecules broke apart, and the atoms recombined with the oxygen to form water and carbon dioxide, as well as char, which is nearly pure carbon, and ash (which is composed of all the inflammable minerals in the paper.)

It was incinerated. Broiled. Cooked. Oxidated. Roasted. Melted. Cremated. Smelted. Toasted. Destroyed.

In other words, it burned. Along with almost everything else I owned.

****

It was March of my senior year of high school, and I was on top of the world. I was graduating in a couple of months, batting .295 on the baseball team, and I was all set to go to Florida the following week for a rip-roarin Spring Break.

It was a Sunday morning. I remember the day of the week because I had planned to wake up and bang out the final draft of my English term paper, due the next day, on Liz's old typewriter.

Some odd popping sounds first made me sit up in bed. (You know how when you're half-asleep, things sound distorted and loud?) I thought nothing of it, and rolled over to get back to dreamland. I fell back asleep (for seconds? Minutes? To this day I have no clue). Then I really woke up, because the popping had gotten intense.

"FIRE!! Get out, it's on fire!" Mom suddenly yelled from the kitchen. I jumped from my bed into the hall–about ten feet–in one mighty leap, and raced towards the kitchen. Behind me I heard Sonny come out of the bathroom, where he'd been having a leisurely soak.

I could tell before I got there that the whole kitchen was ablaze. In the one or two seconds that I was in there, the entire ceiling went *whoooosh*...and I found myself under a roof of flames.

"CALL 911!" Sonny screamed. *Oh my God, my house is burning down. Run. RUN!!* In my peripheral vision I saw Sonny dash under the flames and through the door. "GET OUT!" he said as he went.

To this day, I don't know why I did what I did next. I sprinted to my room, my feet hardly touching the floor. Above my head the flames raced with me. Once inside I yanked open a dresser drawer and grabbed all the clothes inside, then turned around–and faced a wall of fire. I hopped to my knees and crawled, still holding the clothes, through the house and out the door.

Once outside, I looked for Mom. *Where is she!!??* I tore around the side of the house to the kitchen door, but that entire wall was engulfed. "MAAAMAAAAAAA!!" I screamed, and then I saw her. She was on all fours behind a tree in the backyard, howling in disbelief. Wheezing, I ran out to the shoulder of the highway and turned around. With every breath, the air was like lava.

My house—where I had grown up, kissed my first girlfriend, learned to dance, played Nerf basketball with a wicker garbage can as a goal, and become a man—was disappearing before my eyes.

"Well, that's it. She's gone," Sonny said from beside me. His normally ruddy complexion had turned bright pink, and his bald spot had been scorched but good. As we stood there, my mother screaming "Nooooooooo!!" from behind a tree in the backyard, our neighbor Robert ambled over from across the street.

"Yep..." was all he could muster.

"Yep," I said. We watched the crackling blaze in silence.

"Hey. You like your car, do ya?"

"Sure do."

"Well...might wanna move it."

It took me a few seconds to realize what he meant. Our driveway was semi-circular, and my parking spot on the grass between it and the house was now about ten feet from the blaze. I ran to it–fortunately the driver's side was facing away from the fire–and hopped in, sweating like a madman. I drove out of harm's way, then moseyed back over to Sonny and Robert. I could just make out the sirens of the approaching fire trucks.

Then the fireworks began...literally. In my closet was a bag of loot left over from Christmas, with Roman candles and bottle rockets in it. The rockets shot one by one from the heart of the blaze. As we watched the horrible celebration, the National Anthem began running through my head: *And the rocket's red glare / The bombs bursting in air.....*

My house burned for the next two days straight before it gave out.

****

Mom had put some cooking oil on the stove to heat up while she was outside–she was going to cook some chicken for lunch—and had totally forgotten about it. She'd, ah...gotten lost in the joy of gardening. When she glanced at the house, she saw smoke pouring through the kitchen window, and the realization of what was happening slammed into her head.

She ran to the kitchen door and flung it open. When she did, a huge gust of fresh, oxygen-rich air surged into the room, feeding the growing fire. The ceiling was made of a fiberglass compound—extremely flammable—so when the flames found it, it was only a matter of time. A fireman told me later that it was like blowing on the flame in the fireplace to get your living room fire going, only times ten thousand.

When Mom saw that we'd made it out, she ran into the backyard. Across the street, Robert had called the fire department. Since we lived about seven miles from town, it took them about twenty minutes to get there, and by that time it was way too late. They eventually got it under control, but by then there was nothing left.

My room was on the opposite corner from the kitchen, so it hadn't been totally destroyed. Later that afternoon, I remember, I'd peered through my soot-blackened windows, and there was only minor damage. The brand-new high-top sneakers I'd bought the day before had been reduced to piles of rubber on the floor, but it looked like there was some salvageable stuff.

Over the next two days, though, the fire department had to rush back three times, because my room kept reigniting. They finally destroyed everything with their high-pressure hose to make sure.

I stayed with a friend for a few nights afterwards. He was the same size as I was, so in addition to the twelve T-shirts I'd grabbed from my dresser, he had clothes for me to wear. My folks stayed in a friend's tiny trailer down the road for a couple of weeks, since the owner was away on vacation.

For our insurance claim, we had to make a list of everything we owned. If you've ever had to do that, you know it's practically impossible. (Can you honestly say exactly how many pairs of socks you own? I thought not.) Our subsequent shopping trip was almost exciting, in a surreal, dreamlike way. I mean, $1,000 can buy a friggin heap of clothes.

And believe me, I still went to Florida–I wasn't going to let the fact that I'd lost everything I owned stop me from enjoying a week's beachfront debauchery. While there, one night I had an awful nightmare: I dreamed that Mom and I had just returned from shopping. I liked all my new stuff so much that I decided to burn down the house again. Only this time, Mom and Sonny didn't make it out. I awoke screaming.

****

About that term paper: my senior English teacher was a mega-prude named Dr. Park. In addition to being a poster-child for Puritanism, she had recently been relieved of her duties as a professor at a nearby black college. So, in addition to her fuddy-duddiness, she had a chip on her shoulder the size of the NAACP.

I'd had my heart set on doing my paper on Stephen King–I'd been a lifelong fan, reading each of his books as soon as Mom finished them. And she had taken us to see *The Shining* in the theater when I was only 10. 10! I couldn't sleep for weeks, and to this day, I get scared when I see a Big Wheel. But hey...All Work and No Play Makes John a Dull Boy.

Dr. Park flatly refused to let me write about King, saying, "Ah, he's just commercial garbage. Fifty years from now, no one will remember who he is." (Hmmm. Looking back, that statement is so ludicrous I don't know where to begin.) I ended up writing about a local author named Willie Morris instead.

Dr. Park graded our papers as we went– in other words, we received grades on our rough draft, outline, note cards, and so on. Up to that point, I had a high A, so my new plan was to write my final draft based on the outline that was filed squarely away in Dr. Park's desk drawer.

English was first period, so the day after the fire, we filed into her room, people paying me their hushed condolences on the way in. After she called roll, Dr. Park began collecting the term papers. Then she got to the T's.

"Mr. Turner?"

"Ahhhhh.....it's gone."

"What do you mean, 'It's gone'?"

"What do you think I mean? It burned." The other students began shifting nervously in their seats, and my best friend Joe muttered, "Bitch..." under his breath.

"Now John, how could it have *burned*? Gracious..."

She didn't know about the fire. As fast as news traveled, it hadn't made its way to her. So I told her. When I had finished, she turned bright red and was silent for a few seconds, then said quietly, "I'm sorry." Maybe my imagination was playing tricks on me, but I think she even choked back tears.

After class, she pulled me aside and told me she would give me two weeks to do it again.

"Two weeks? I can do it in two *days*. Just give me the outline, and–"

"No, I mean two weeks to do it again. All of it."

Holy Christ. "But–but I've done all but the f–"

"Mr. Turner, completing a thesis is a process. One that must follow a logical course. I'm sorry, but you'll start over from the beginning."

At that point, I thought of my options: a) cut her head off with a butter knife, or b) just suck it up and do what she asked. For obvious reasons, I chose option b.

And I finished it. I worked many late nights in that tiny borrowed trailer, and had more nightmares (about Willie Morris *himself* setting my house on fire), but I finished it.

Dr. Park gave me a B. "It was messy, disorganized, and poorly planned," she said. "The content is acceptable, I guess, but it's...well, rushed is the most appropriate word."

Jeez, you heartless bitch, I wonder why. I didn't say that to her, though now I wish I had. When Mom found out about it, she flipped. She had an impromptu meeting with Dr. Park, Miss Huff, our guidance counselor, and Mr. Mayo, the principal. Mom refused to tell me what had gone down at that meeting, but when I got my next report card, I had an A+ in English.

****

A few weeks later, I graduated. It was bittersweet, but mostly I was just thankful to be alive. The day after the ceremony, I sat on the brand-new couch in our brand-new double-wide trailer—all courtesy of Nationwide Insurance—and looked out the window at the blackened shell of my house. My folks had put the trailer about fifty yards from it, and its two remaining brick walls were perfectly framed by the trailer's living-room window.

My memory of what happened next is dim. I rushed out the front door and around the house, and I grabbed our new sledgehammer. Then I jogged down to the nearest wall, and I began screaming.

I tore into one wall, then the other, without mercy. It took me thirty minutes to knock them both down with the sledgehammer, but when I had finished...I was *done*. With the house, with my anger, with my sadness, with my loss. I went back up to the trailer and slept for two days. When I woke up, I was ready to start the next act.

INTERLUDE:
A Little Cane Pain

One day I was walking on the sidewalk from the bus stop to my office, when snap!! My cane literally split in two. I tumbled ass-first onto the walk. I wasn't hurt, but I looked like one of the idiots I make fun of every chance I get. (Karma, maybe?)

I was right next to the bakery across the street from my office, a place I visited on a daily basis, so I hobbled in and they duct-taped my shit right up.

Thing is my former cane was metal, a shiny blue deal an old girlfriend had bought for me for like $100. Apparently some pin holding it all together broke. So now I'm back to my cheap chrome model.

I'm sure if I think really hard, I can figure out a way to blame it on Obamacare. Caaaaaaanes!!!!

16. THE TALE OF SHERRY DRAKE
(1997)

(Soundtrack: STRAY CATS—"Sexy & 17")

In the world of office politics, it was the equivalent of assassinating the president. My inability to see my place in that particular pecking order was ridiculously apparent. To get right down to brass tacks: I used absolutely no common sense the day I called my boss a bitch.

****

In the months following my graduation from college, I became a slave. I didn't pick cotton or get whipped, but some days, I swear, I knew what that must have felt like. I was working at a restaurant in my college town in Mississippi, and the place was undoubtedly the most popular joint around. It was owned by a guy named Nick Karpinski, who'd been a linebacker for the Pittsburgh Steelers in the 1960s. The restaurant was run by his son and daughter, two of the kindest people you'd ever want to meet.

And Nick himself...well, he was a bear with a heart of gold. Besides yelling "GET TO WORK!!" in random employees' faces with a maniacal grin plastered on his own mug, he had an odd but effective way of putting the fear of God into every new hire.

On their first day there, he would lead them around the restaurant, screaming in their ears like a drill sergeant. If they could take it— which a few of them couldn't, scampering out the door with their tails between their legs—he'd laugh and say, "Aw, I'm just kidding, Sugar Bear!" (Sugar Bear was his pet name for everyone he knew.) Then, after their shift was done, he'd buy them all the beer they could drink in the bar upstairs.

People around town couldn't get enough of our cozy Southern atmosphere and our rich, delectable food. There was a core group of about seven of us that kept the place going, and we all did a little bit of everything; I worked in the kitchen, the bar, and the dining room— sometimes all on the same night. Needless to say, we were close-knit, and because of our shared dedication, there was always a line out the door.

And then, one day, it all came crashing down.

One of our regular customers was a man named John Drake. He was a local personal injury lawyer, and he was *made* of money. The combination of overaffluence and overfamiliarity with the law put him among the hungriest of the power-hungry, a complete jerk. He'd recently married his fourth wife, who was as snotty as he was, and one night they sat down to dinner in my section.

John Drake was every waiter's

nightmare. The moment he and his new wife were seated, he started snapping his fingers at any server who walked by. "Hey, hey! We need some drinks here. Hey you! Drinks over here!!" From the back of the dining room, I saw them at the table.

Christ…Just what I need. Might as well introduce myself as Kunta Kinte. I plastered on my waiter's grin and went over. And true to form, the Drakes ran me ragged. His wife, Sherry, was drinking wine like she had a grape deficiency, and they made me pick their live lobsters out of the tank myself, directing me from the table without even getting up.

"No, I want that one. The one next to it. Jesus, boy, the big red one!" Drake shouted across the dining room as I chased the shellfish around the tank with a net. I began mentally hawking up the huge wad of snot I wanted to spit in his soup.

A few minutes later, though, when I exited the kitchen to serve them their escargot, I was knocked flat. Sitting at the table with them was the most beautiful girl I'd ever seen. I approached the table nervously and set down the snails.

"Something to drink, ma'am?" I asked the young goddess. She looked mischievously at Mrs. Drake.

"Can I have a glass of wine, Mom?"

"No, Rachel, you know you've got that big English test in the morning."

Ah, nothing I love better than a fresh young co-ed, I thought. When her gorgeous blue eyes met mine, the sparks were almost visible, and I could feel my battalion of hormones preparing for a fiery skirmish.

"Ah, English exam, huh? Is that your major, English?" I asked the goddess.

"It might be. I don't start till next year. I've still got a year left in high school."

Retreat, RETREAT! "Oh...well, best of luck to you." I took her drink order—a soda—and continued with their meal. *Damn. Don't even think about going there. You know what they say—fifteen'll get you twenty.*

Discouraged, I went on with my shift, purposefully averting my eyes whenever I headed towards the Drakes' table. Yet I could've sworn Rachel was staring at me with the old "Do Me Now" look. *Down, boy!*

Just after I had served the Drakes their coffee, the front door swung open, and in walked Nick Karpinski. "Hey folks!" he said to no one in particular. Then, seeing John Drake, his face lit up.

"JOHN DRAKE!! Hey there, Sugar Bear!" he yelled, walking over. From the kitchen I saw him sit at their table. *Jeez...perfect.* I just sucked it up, reaffixed my grin, and got on with it.

An hour or so later, Nick was still there. From the snatches of conversation I overheard, they were talking business. And then, as I lingered nearby tidying up my other tables, Drake lowered the boom.

"So Nick, let me ask you somethin kinda personal. How much you reckon this place is worth?"

"Aw, Sugar Bear, you know I'm not gonna kiss and tell," Nick answered, smiling.

"But if you had to guess...would you say bout a million?"

"Oh, at least."

"Well, Sherry and I have been talkin...and we decided we're gonna buy this place. I'll write you a check for a million and a quarter right now."

I felt the hairs on the back of my neck stand up. *C'mon, Karpinksi, don't do it! Be a man. Be a linebacker, for God's sake!!*

Nick let out a long, bellowing laugh. Finally he said gravely, "You....you can't be serious."

Mrs. Drake squealed, "I was a hostess in a place just like this. And I loved it! Ever since, I've dreamed about owning my own restaurant. And now, with John's mon—-help, I can make it happen! Oh Nick, just think about it, would you?"

"Sherry, there's nothin to think about. I love this place. I can't pull the plug just like that. No...the answer's no." *You tell em, Sugar Bear!*

"Well, it's a standin offer. So if you ever change your mind..." Drake said.

"Well, I won't. This place means too much."

The Drakes stood to go. "Well, arright then...but it's your loss." Drake snapped his fingers in my direction. "Hey, hey boy, how much we owe?"

"Aw, you go on. This one's on me," Nick said. As I watched the Drakes say their goodbyes and leave, I resisted the urge to hug Nick and thank him for not selling the place to those ogres.

Sadly, I would see a lot more of the Drakes in the near future.

****

The next day when I arrived for the dinner shift, Nick was standing in the dining room as I came in the door. And standing next to him was Sherry Drake. I felt my bowels loosen.

"Uh, John, I want you to meet your new boss," Nick said. "She and John just bought the place. Signed the papers this mornin."

I quit. Aloud I said, "Congratulations. It'll be nice to work with you."

"Well, it'll be nice to have you working for me!" she chirped. *Seriously, I quit.* "I'll tell ya, there are gonna be some changes around here, but I'll just watch how things work till I catch on." That was the first time I truly saw her for what she really was: Evil Incarnate.

I looked at Nick, who just shrugged as if to say, *Hey, she's your boss now....* I had to know why.

"Nick, can I ask what made you decide to sell this place?"

"FLORIDA, boy!! The wife and I are movin there as soon as the sale goes through."
So...the Sugar Bear isn't such a bear after all.

"Well, we're gonna miss you."

"I'll miss you too, boy." There was an awkward silence. "I gotta go. But Sherry, you remember what I told ya–these people are like family. Treat em that way. That's what keeps the folks comin back for dinner."

"I know, Nick," she said sweetly, but I could tell what she was really thinking: *These employees aren't family, you Polish oaf....they're peons.* My *peons.* Nick walked out the door, and I never saw him again.

Sherry turned to me. "Okay, let's get started. Go get your section ready."

My God, my God, why hast thou shat upon me? "But Sherry, we–"

"Miss Drake."

Christ. "Miss Drake...we always get the whole dining room ready at closing time the night before. The whole place is ready to go."

"Then you'll check it again. That's the way things are gonna be around here from now on. You're here to *work,*" she said like she was talking to a 10-year-old. Looking back, I should've quit right then and there, because it only got worse. *Exponentially* worse.

Over the next several days, Sherry managed to make enemies out of every single person who worked there. She'd stand at the end of the bar on busy nights and talk to the bartender, trying to learn what was in each drink. "What's that you're making?" "Easy with the gin! That's way too much."

She made us count our sugar packets. I still remember it exactly: Ten regulars, eight Sweet n' Lows, and five Equals, in that order. Anyone caught altering the sugar system would be called into her office for a talking-to. That was for the first offense. I don't think anyone did it twice.

She would stand in the kitchen and yell at the cooks: "Let's go! Where's that order of crab legs!?" or "Jesus! How long does it take a well-done steak to cook!?" I'm surprised nobody plunged a chef's knife into her chest.

After about two weeks, everything began to unravel. One day, when I got to work, who should be there...but Rachel. The goddess.

It was her eighteenth birthday that day, and she and I went out to celebrate after my shift. She spent the night at my house. I didn't realize until I got to work the next day what a horrible mistake I'd made.

When I walked in, another waiter, Clem, came up to me like I was his hero.

"Hey, it's *Chester!* Way to go, man! Gimme some skin!" He held out his hand. Just then, I heard someone call my name.

"John!" It was Drake, and he and Sherry were standing at the kitchen door, scowling.

Oh, Lord. I walked up to them, smiling innocently. "What's going on?"

"Boy, you *know* what's going on!" Drake hissed.

"Rachel came home at *10 this morning!!*" Miss Drake yelled. "When I asked where she'd been, she told me all about how she stayed at your house. She's just a child! Oh, I'm so mad I could scream!"

"I...I'm sorry." I didn't know what else to tell them.

"I know you are!! A sorry excuse for a human being, that's what you are! Just....just get out of my sight!" I turned beet-red and went through the kitchen door.

Was I mad? Oh, boy. "Mad" doesn't even begin to describe it. As I went around to my tables trying to look busy, one phrase kept flashing in my head: *Sorry excuse for a human being.... Sorry excuse for a human being....* I quietly plotted my revenge.

At five o'clock the dining room opened, and since it was Saturday, the restaurant was full in minutes. I went to the center of the dining room and called Miss Drake over.

"Sherry! Sherry, come here a second." She marched over to where I stood.

"You know you're supposed to call me Miss Drake! Now what do you want? And make it quick!"

Well, here goes nothing. Just do it. DO IT!

"You're a bitch," I said.

She froze, and for a few seconds she looked confused. "What did you just say?"

"I said you're a bitch!" I raised my voice to be heard by everyone in the room. "You waltz in here and start ordering people around like you have any idea of what's going on. You were a friggin *hostess*, for chrissakes! The people who work here, and all these people too–" I gestured to the diners–"We all love this place. It is–*was*–our home. Not anymore. And it's because of you, bitch." I untied my apron and tossed it in her direction. "I bet this place'll close down in a month. But you know what? I won't be around to see it, thank God." I walked towards the front door. The place was silent. I opened the door, then turned around. Sherry–and everybody else–just stood there, slackjawed.

"Oh yeah...your daughter Rachel? Best lay I ever had." I walked out, and the door swung shut behind me.

****

That was the first time I'd ever *really* told someone off, and it felt great. Until the end of the month, that is, when all my bills were due and I had no way to pay them. Since I'd been a theatre major, I figured I'd make the most of the opportunity and find a job as an actor. I accepted a position with the theater company in upstate New York, and moved there full of hopes and dreams.

Oh, Sherry Drake was a bitch, no doubt about it. But some things are just better left unsaid.

INTERLUDE:
The Blind Leading the Stupid [Reprise]

Not long ago I went to the convenience store to pick up some ground coffee, and as I got out of my buddy Mike's truck to go in, some homeless-looking dude standing next to the door was staring at me quizzically.

I had my shades on. As I shuffled to the door, he held it open for me–not an unusual occurrence–and as I passed him he said loudly, "Hey buddy! Can you see?"

Jesus Christ. I told him I could see only a little, and I was looking for coffee.

"What kind?"

"Whatever's cheapest," I said to the wall next to him. I expected him to scoot ahead of me to the coffee aisle, but as I took off my sunglasses to go grab a can, he went to the fresh coffee urns.

When I finally got in line with a can of Folger's in my hand–and my shades resting on top of my head–I felt a tap on my shoulder. I turned, and there he stood with a full cup of joe.

"Here's some coffee. Hey...think you could by me a beer?"

What do you do in these situations? Especially at 10 in the morning? I took the high road and told him to grab a six-pack. He came back with a sixer of Red Dog tall boys.

Fuck a buncha Starbucks–that was the

best seven-dollar cup of coffee I've ever had.

17. COWS IN THE YARD!! (2006)

(Soundtrack: STEELY DAN—"Black Cow")

This one's a perfect instance of déjà vu all over again.

After a yet another devastating argument with my fiancée, we'd decided that splitting up was the best (and only) course of action. Numb, I went to stay with my best friend until I could get back on my feet. During my couple of months there, the story ideas flowed like water; I think I was in such shock that my brain used its creativity as a defense mechanism, so my output increased exponentially.

I'd recently finished "Pigs in the Yard," which, even before it was written down, had people shaking their heads in disbelief: "You mean...your mother shot three pigs? Because they were in her *flower bed*!?" The incident was fodder for many a belly-laugh; even now, I can scarcely believe my luck at having witnessed it.

One afternoon, I took a break from writing and checked my email. After slogging through the spam, I opened one from my crazy pig-shootin mother.

I had to re-read it several times, pinching myself to make sure I wasn't dreaming. Having recently relived the pig incident through writing about it, I had a hard time wrapping my brain around this one. In fact, I had to have her tell me the whole story again that night on the phone:

Mom was "on the potty," as she had put it in the email, when she heard Sonny bellow downstairs.

"OH, MY GOD!"

"What is it?" she called out, worried that he'd had a heart attack. No answer. She finished her business and rushed downstairs.

"Are you in here?" she asked the empty living room. Still no response. She went into the bedroom, fearing the worst. Finally she heard Sonny in the closet, loading his shotgun.

"I'll shoot em before I let em trample up our yard!" he growled, rushing past her out the door with the gun.

As she turned to see where he was going, she looked out of the window as eight huge cows emerged from the azalea bed and trotted around the corner of the house. They were Brangus cows, bred from Brahma and Angus, and they were the size of compact cars. They galloped down the hill towards the pond, with the dog, Black Bear, barking his head off in hot pursuit.

BOOM! BOOM BOOM!

(In my mind's eye, I could see Sonny frozen on the porch in his shooter's stance, just as Mom had been in hers twenty years before.)

Since the shotgun was loaded with number 6 shells—"bird shot"—the blasts, on target though they were, were like horsefly bites to the cows. They continued down the hill,

Mom said, the hindmost cow stopping to leave a huge cowpie in some freshly planted elephant ears. Black Bear, upon hearing the first blast, turned and ran, tail tucked, back around the house.

The beasts milled around the lake, drank some pond-water, then ambled back up the hill and around the house. They went as if they knew exactly what they were doing, as if they knew they were in total control. Mom and Sonny just watched incredulously from the porch. It was the only thing they could do.

****

Mom said in her email that the owner of the adjacent property had had a tree fall onto his fence, allowing his cows to make their escape. Mom spent the next couple of hours on the phone tracking the guy down. He agreed to fix the fence, and by nightfall the Bovine Wall was whole again.

It all happened just as Mom told me in the email and on the phone. Even now, I'm having a hard time believing it. I mean, Jesus. What's next? What farm animals are left to shoot??

I'm still waiting on the harried phone call from her during which she tells me that she had no choice but to kill the goats that were munching on her brand-new Buick LaCrosse.

At this point, that would be par for the

course.

INTERLUDE:
Cart Rage

Because of my disability, I use one of those electric carts when I grocery-shop. And I wanna tell you about cart rage.

It happens every time I go. Some people, old ladies usually, shop like they're the only people in the store. While I sit impatiently waiting for them to move out of the way of the milk, they just take their own sweet time.... They examine each carton like it's some outer-space artifact.

Hmmmmmm......I wonder when this one expires? Let me look at all the other ones. Maybe there's a fresher jug. Hmmmmmm......

Christ. They're ALL THE SAME, you waste of space!! Fucking MOOOVE!!!

What's worse, they're often hard of hearing too. So when I say "Excuse me..." over and over with my impaired speech, they usually look at me after a few seconds and just nod, like "Howya doin?" They haven't heard a word I've said. FUCK.

So when you hear about some crippled guy crushing an old lady's pelvis with his Power Chair.....you'll know I couldn't take it anymore.

18. 88 KEYS AND FOUR HEROES (1982-present)

(Soundtrack: TRADITIONAL—"Merrily We Roll Along")

"I'll toil for my woman, I'll sweat for the kids
Working till I'm wrinkled and I'm gray....
While that lucky old sun, has nothin to do
But roll around heaven all day...."

As a boy of 12, I remember Sonny dancing and singing at the top of his lungs to that tune: "Lucky Old Sun," covered by the Wild One himself, Jerry Lee Lewis.

Sonny and Jerry Lee were distant cousins, so I spent my teens listening to "Chantilly Lace" and "Crazy Arms." I passed many a Saturday night with Sonny, drinking beer and listening to Jerry Lee sing "Over the Rainbow," while Sonny told me about growing up in South Louisiana.

It was during these sticky, rowdy nights that I fell in love with the piano. Its versatility—percussive, lyrical, colorful, and rhythmic all at once–gave me feelings towards music I'd previously left untapped. And a genius like Jerry Lee Lewis... "He just made that pie-anuh talk to ya, boy," as Sonny would say.

I think it was Sonny's Cajun influence as much as anything else that started my love affair with the keyboards. He tells of an uncle of his,

Vince Tuminello, who owned a nightclub where Jerry Lee would play. The bar itself was horseshoe-shaped, and Jerry Lee would advertise for it on the radio: "C'mon up one side and down the other...at Tuminello's!" Listening to Sonny's tales, I daydreamed of neon, smoke, and a stretch of black-and-white keys, covered in the sweat, blood, and joy of countless dudes.

Lucky for us, there was always a piano in the house. Around age 10, I'd sit and watch Liz play "Fur Elise" or Chicago's "Color My World," and soon, I was plinking out "Mary Had a Little Lamb." I found that I learned a song better by playing what *sounded* right, rather than trying to follow the sheet music. I couldn't figure out how to look at both the music and the keyboards at the same time, so learning by ear was the method I preferred. And soon enough, I was playing well enough that my sisters stopped saying, "C'mon, brat!" every time I sat down to play.

Fast-forward a few years: I was a college sophomore, dating a Piano major, and had recently discovered jazz. Real jazz, like Coltrane and Miles Davis. I'd started dabbling in music theory—the "math" of music, some call it— when I heard about a young New Orleans singer/pianist named Harry Connick, Jr., who'd just released the soundtrack to *When Harry Met Sally*.

The first time I heard him sing and play,

I was forever a changed man.

****

"Meet me on the corner of close and soon
I'll have a song in my head, and my hands on a
tune...
If nothin lasts forever, then I figure I better
Take you forever, for now..."

That song, "Forever, For Now," is from Harry's first album of original material, *We Are in Love.* He's a Renaissance man for sure–actor, singer, bandleader, and one hell of a piano player.

When *When Harry Met Sally* came out, I instantly fell in love–with the music and the man. (No, I'm not gay. But if I were...oh, my.) I locked myself in a practice room with my Walkman, and it took me over a week (and about a case of batteries) to learn "Don't Get Around Much Anymore." Of course, it wasn't even close to Harry's version, but I knew the basics of the tune. And you know what? I learned more about how to play piano in that one week than I have before or since.

I took private lessons for one semester, but I never really got past "Merrily We Roll Along." My instructor, Mr. Davis, was in fact gay. I mean Liberace-gay. (I even considered bringing a fire extinguisher to my lessons.) "No, no, NO!" he'd yell at me, slapping my hand with his limp wrist whenever I'd revert to my "self-learnt" techniques. When I'd slip and look at the keys instead of the music, he'd angrily push my chin back up. (Amazing how, mad as he was, he did even that with homosexual flair.)

So that was the end of my private tutelage. Although I might've ended up a better player had I stuck with the lessons, I just didn't feel right pecking out "Little Brown Jug" with my eyes glued to the sheet music. I got more joy out of playing what I wanted the *way* I wanted, rather than the way someone else had written it.

So on with college I went, spending more and more time in the practice room with my Walkman. One of my fondest memories of those endless hours is when my girlfriend, watching me bang out "It Had to Be You," remarked, "Oh my, this is sooo sexy..." It made me feel like I was Harry himself.

Once I'd moved to upstate New York to work for a children's theatre company, I was picked to be the company's musical director, and had recently begun dating yet another musician. She was talented as hell, and turned me on to all sorts of new artists.

When I discovered Steely Dan, it was all over.

****

"The danger on the rocks is surely past

Still I remain tied to the mast....
Could it be that I have found my home at last,
Home at last...."

That's the chorus to "Home at Last," from the Dan's juggernaut 1977 album *Aja*. I'd previously listened to these nerd-rock icons with surface amusement, but after a few feeble attempts at songwriting for the theatre company, I was more aware of the "mechanics" of a tune. Armed with my newfound musical wisdom, I bought a Steely Dan songbook.

This is no joke: I got through the third measure of "FM," the first song in the book, before I just gave up. I learned one undeniable fact: in addition to being incredibly ear-friendly, Steely Dan's tunes are impossible to play. The neurotic perfectionism and disdain for musical "norms" of Donald Fagen and Walter Becker, the Dan's founders, have made them two of the top rock n' roll musicians ever. And if you don't agree with me, that's fine. I could care less–an opinion I'm sure Steely Dan shares with me.

So, after trying (and failing) to reach anywhere near their level of musical savvy, I resigned myself to loving them from afar. (But I proudly played those first three measures of "FM" for anyone who'd listen.)

I played them until May 17, 2002. That's the day I quit playing the piano forever.

****

On that fine spring night, an evil man took much of my life away. Because of the beating he gave me, I can no longer walk without assistance. When I speak, people usually ask, "What'd you say?" My balance sucks, I can't play video games, or sing, or ride a bicycle, or act, or even hold a pencil in my left hand, which is the hand I used to write with. I typed the sentence you're now reading with one finger of my right hand.

And I'm no longer able to play those three measures of "FM." Same goes for "Don't Get Around Much Anymore." Hell, I can't even struggle through "Merrily We Roll Along."

Believe me, I tried. I spent countless hours in front of my Yamaha, trying to plink out simple scales. But the muscles in my hands just don't do what my brain tells them to anymore. After weeks of frustration and sadness, I sold the Yamaha for a fraction of its worth.

One thing that evil man left me with, though, is my spirit. I may not create music the way I used to...but I still revel in the joy it brings. In the end, isn't that what music does, anyway?

I can, however, play the *hell* out of an air piano. Jerry Lee, Harry, Steely Dan...nothing's out of reach. I'm especially good in the car, where I use the dashboard as my keyboard. The driver will ask, "What the hell are you doing?"

Most times I don't answer; I'm lost in the spirit of the music.

INTERLUDE:
'Asshole' is Not a Handicap

Here's another confession (and this is the very definition of karma taking a ginormous bite outta my crippled ass):

One day when I was in college, I had to run into the mall real quick, but I couldn't find a parking place. So I parked right up front in a handicapped space. (Hey, I was only gonna be inside for five minutes! Gimme a break, right?) But just as I was getting out of my car, a cop rolled by real slow, frowning suspiciously at me.

So...I started walking all spastic-like, trying my best to imitate the guy with multiple sclerosis I'd known growing up. (And know what? It probably wasn't very dissimilar to the way I walk now.) The cop rolled on, and as soon as he was gone I reverted to my assholish, look-what-I-just-got-away-with swagger and virtually skipped to the mall entrance.

So, as I was leaving the grocery store recently, pushing my cart full of groceries to where my trike was parked in the bicycle parking area, I noticed two "tourons" —that's Key West-speak for tourist-morons—sitting in their golf cart eating lunch. And the golf cart was parked in a handicapped space.

The space was right next to the bike area, so as I put my groceries in my trike basket, I started looking over at them with the most evil stare I could muster. (And during this time, they both got out of the cart at some point and started walking around, so they didn't seem to be physically disabled at all.)

One of the tourons finally acknowledged my evil stare. "Uh, you got a problem?"

Oh, it's on. I grabbed my cane and shuffled towards them. "Yes, I do. You realize you're parked in a handicapped space, right?"

"Fuck you, man...we're leaving in a minute." At that his touron buddy snickered.

I got an idea. "Oh, okay." Grinning, I pulled out my cell, pretended to dial, then proceeded to have the following *faux* chat with Key West Police Chief Donie Lee:

"Yes, Chief Lee, please...it's John Turner...Hey, Chief Lee! It's John. You know, your HANDICAPPED FRIEND? Oh, fine...listen, I'm here in the Publix parking lot, and there are two smartasses parked in a handicapped spot..."

By this time, the tourons were backing out to leave, cursing me the whole time. (I'm surprised one of them didn't actually shake his fist at me.) So I got on my trike and rode home pleased as punch.

I myself didn't need that handicapped spot. But some other disabled person might have. And when I ride the bus these days, I like to act as The Enforcer, politely asking able-bodied people sitting right beneath the "This Seat Reserved for Handicapped or Senior

Passengers" sign to move so that I or other disabled/senior folks can sit down closer to the exit.

Why do I do these things, you ask? I think it's for two reasons. One, I will forever try to redeem myself for the horrendous stunt I pulled in college; and two, I just think that assholes need to be put in their place from time to time.

Boy, I sure wish I had been.

19. THE ULTIMATE SYNC MOMENT
(1999)

(Soundtrack: ROLLING STONES—
"Sympathy for the Devil")

Hopefully, everybody on Earth has two or three of these happen during their lifetime: Those instances when it seems like all the planets line up and you become one with the universe.

And c'mon, I'm not talking about that great acid trip you had in college (though those were indeed fun). It just seems to me that, every once in a while, God decides to send down a blessing by having several unrelated things line up perfectly. A "sync moment," I like to call it. It can start as simply as the rhythm of your windshield wipers *exactly* matching up with the beat of the song on the radio.

Well, I experienced the *ultimate* sync moment. It involved four creative people, the Rolling Stones, a rural highway, and some road construction workers.

For about seven minutes—or whatever the length of the Stones' "Sympathy for the Devil"—a whole lot of stuff lined up: The song, the road, miscellaneously chosen percussion instruments, and our minds all simply meshed.

****

I'd moved to my town, nestled in the

Finger Lakes region of upstate New York, just a few weeks before to work for a well-known educational theatre company. It was a year-long gig going to schools all over the state and performing plays for different grade levels.

Each play dealt with what the students were learning in school that year. The fourth-grade show, for example, was about Native Americans, because fourth-graders in New York are required by the Learning Standards to study the Iroquois.

Anyway, we got to do classroom workshops about the subject matter before each show, and we were trained beforehand to give our 30-minute lectures extremely effectively—each one was basically a half-hour monologue that the students just adored.

For me, it was the best of both worlds—teaching *and* performing. People's undivided attention and adoration all day, every day? For *pay*? Are you kidding me? It was heaven.

But the summer gig, which I was doing at the time, was different. (And by different, I mean it was so easy I felt guilty cashing my weekly paychecks.) The tour consisted of a one-act children's play that we performed at parks or playgrounds in the area. Almost every show was local, which meant we rarely had to leave for a gig before 8 a.m.

But towards the end of the run, we had a show in the Catskills, which was about a four-hour drive. It was scheduled to start at 9 in the morning, which meant we would leave at 4.

4 a.m. The time when some folks—for years, me included—are still partying from the night before. And now I had to take a trip across the state to be Mr. Super-Nice-Actor-Guy for a bunch of kids? I was scared.

Our trip was to take us a looong way down Route 17, a rural highway that runs from Binghamton to New York City, passing through next to nothing. And it was on Route 17 that the magic happened.

****

During the school year, each show toured for a couple of months, and I got to spend many hours on what seemed like every road in central New York. We'd usually go to two schools per day, some as far as three hours away from our town, so I went to just about every shit burg within 150 or so miles.

After a while, we tour members, of which there were about a dozen, figured out a rating system: Each place was scored on the quality and/or quantity of its eating establishments. Since we'd often be booked at two schools in the same town, we got to know each town and its eateries quite well.

There was The 69er Diner in a tiny town called Candor. I have no clue as to why it was named that—maybe the owners just wanted to have some fun while living up to their town's name. Who knows? The place had crappy food but...hey. How often can you say, "I ate at The 69er," and mean it literally?

There was also the Foursome Diner in Fulton. It was a hole-in-the-wall that had maybe five tables, and the food was horrible. No lie: When I ordered a crock of French onion gratinee, the waitress brought me a bowl of cold beef broth with raw onions in it and a slice of unmelted Swiss cheese on top.

I ate a bag of M & M's for lunch instead, but at least I can now proudly proclaim that I ate at the Foursome.

And of course, with that sort of diet comes some otherworldly gastric repercussions. At the risk of being disgusting, I have to admit I have destroyed almost every school bathroom in Central New York. (Is it wrong to be proud of that? Probably so.)

The most memorable occasion was in Cortland. We'd gotten to the school after leaving another diner, where I'd eaten a patty melt for lunch for what must have been the fourth day in a row. I had a few minutes to kill between my workshops and the show, so I went into the kindergarten bathroom to, ah, do my "duty."

Once the "kids were in the pool," I waded through the brown mirage from the toilet to the sink to wash my hands. Then the door opened, and a kid of about 6 walked in. After a second a look of both confusion and disgust crossed his face.

"What...what happened, mister?" he asked while he pinched his nostrils shut with his tiny fingers.

"Well, I just went to the bathroom!" I chirped, trying to be cheerful despite the dry-heaves I felt coming on; I thought this must be how death smells.

Apparently the kid thought so, too. "Well..." He crossed to the open window. "I wonder...that must be coming from outside." He stood on his tiptoes to peer out the window. "Is something dead out there?"

It was all I could do not to explode with laughter. "Maybe so." I made my escape to the hall.

Before the show—an assembly for grades K-2—we actors were sitting on the edge of the stage as the students filed in. The kid from the bathroom and his classmates ended up in the front row.

"Hey, that's him!" the kid whispered to his friends when he saw me. "That's the Stinky Man!"

They all took a deep breath, apparently trying to get a whiff of any lingering death-odor. "Nu-uuhhhh," one of them said. "I don't smell him now."

After the show, we were moving some set pieces out to our van when the kids saw me from down the hallway.

"Goodbye, Stinky Man!!" they yelled in

unison, then ran away laughing.

I will never forget the impact I must've had on their young lives.

****

On our way to the Catskills that summer day, my fellow tour member Mike drove until Binghamton, then I got behind the wheel. It was about 5:30.

As any frequent traveler knows, on long trips the radio is your lifeline. And because of the hilly terrain surrounding Route 17, we lost all radio reception about 30 miles after leaving Binghamton.

We sang a few songs, but quickly got bored with that, and settled for being miserable. At one point I hit the Scan button on the radio, but it just kept cycling through the entire dial without finding any stations.

As the sun was rising, we came to some ongoing road construction, with bumps in the road every 100 feet or so, orange barrels along the shoulder, and crews about every quarter-mile.

The radio continued its never-ending scan. "Jeez..." sighed Andrea, another tour member, from the back seat.

"–troduce myself, I'm a man of wealth and taste...." Mick Jagger was suddenly singing. The radio had found a station. Boy, had it ever.

"Yeeeaaaahhhh!!" we all yelled.

"Sympathy for the Devil!" We all sang along with Mick. And eerily, the "bump....bump...." of the van going over the construction matched *perfectly* with the beat.

The key to the van was on a huge ring with about 30 other keys on it, so I hunched over the wheel and started jingling the ring for percussion. Laughing hysterically, Andrea, Mike and Joey joined in by tapping on an empty soda bottle with a pencil, dragging a pen over the edge of a comb, or pounding on the van ceiling.

When the song came to the chorus, the Stones singing "Hoo hooooo! Hoo hooooo!" over and over, I started blowing the horn to match the refrain.

"Beep beeeeep! (Jingle jingle jingle) Beep beeep! (Jingle jingle jingle)..." We were like a rolling rock group as we breezed down the road. I found that if I kept my speed at exactly 62 miles per hour, the construction bumps stayed perfectly synchronized with the tune. Whenever we passed a construction crew, they'd either smile and wave or stare quizzically in response to the "beep beeeep" of the horn.

After the song ended, the station played for a few more minutes until we lost reception again. And we didn't get another station until just before we reached our destination.

But it didn't matter. We were all so high from that perfect sync moment, the silence was appropriate and beautiful. And our show that morning was the best one of the run.

If you haven't already done this, listen immediately to "Sympathy for the Devil," if you have a copy. I think you'll have a whole new appreciation for it. I know I did.

INTERLUDE: A Letter to Natsu

Dear Natsu,

Thanks. Remember? You took me for some drunk asshole with money–which I actually was, at least that night, anyway–and almost killed me for it. The worst thing about it? Typing with one fucking hand.

But you know what? That beatdown was the best thing ever. Not the month I spent in a coma, or the walking with a cane...or even the fact that I have to collect Social Security Disability because I no longer have the physical capabilities to perform a profession that took me years to learn.

Because of you, I had to re-invent myself. And said beatdown rocks because...now I wake up every day literally happy to be alive. I've come to realize that family, friends, doing what you love to do— there's no substitute for them. What I'm trying to say is that, unfortunately for you, almost dying will give a guy a TON of perspective.

Though this probably won't happen, I hope that during your years in prison you figure out how precious life is. In the meantime...you know what keeps me going? Knowing I'm not you.

Hoping you enjoy the anal rape,
John

20. THE REASON FOR KEY WEST (2012)

(previously published in the October 2013 issue of "The AA Grapevine")

(Soundtrack: PHILLIP PHILLIPS—"Home")

"Things happen for a reason."

If you're like me, you hear somebody say that about once a week. And if you consider what the phrase truly means...well, there could be as many interpretations of it as there are brands of Russian vodka.

To me, the phrase's meaning has to do with a combination of karma and omnipotence. Past circumstances cause any event, whether great or small, but it's all controlled by God (or Jehovah, or Yahweh, Allah, Sam Walton...whatever your personal moniker for the Supreme Being). In other words, everything that happens is a result of previous events, but all the events are under God's control. (That's all the explanation I'm good for. Already I'm leaking brain matter out my damn ears.)

On the morning of January 3, 2012, little did I know how meaningful those words would come to be. That day I boarded a plane in my hometown of Jackson, Miss., my eventual destination being Key West, Fla. I was going to visit Patrick, one of my oldest friends and a decade-long Key West resident, to a) get as wasted as I could, and b) run from the mountain of problems in my life.

But in hindsight, it seems as if God brought me to Key West for something a little different.

****

Here's the deal: I am, without any shadow of doubt, a colossal alcoholic. For the last 25 years or so, from the time I started filching leftover beers out of the back of my stepdad's pickup truck when I was 16, alcohol has ruled me. And my buddy Johnny Barleycorn has been the source of allllllllll those aforementioned problems: DUIs. Jail. Rehab. Broken relationships. Lost jobs. Evictions. And on and on and on...

(Oh, yeah. I got beaten almost to death by a guy I met in a bar. There's that too.)

I'll start this one *in medias res*: I went home to Mississippi for the holidays last December, after an ugly breakup with my girlfriend. I'd moved in with her in Brooklyn the previous summer, and our entire six-month relationship was a disaster.

I'd told Patrick about a month before that I might be showing up at his place after the New Year, and he said that was fine; we'd seen each other only once in the twenty years since we left school. I'd given him the impression that I'd just be visiting, but honestly, I didn't have anywhere else to go. Patrick and I had been roommates and close friends during college, and in addition to learning how to party like rock stars, we shared extremely similar outlooks on life. So he welcomed me with open arms...at first.

When I got there, the welcome party lasted four or five days. I don't remember much about that time, other than hazy memories of making out with some chick I'd never met right there on the sidewalk in front of Pat's house, and both pissing and puking on the couch where I passed out (none of which were new experiences).

But after our mini-vacation was over, Patrick came back down to Earth and went back to work at the strip club where he's the featured DJ. (And stop right there. Despite what you might think, Pat works incredibly hard, no pun intended, with long, sweaty hours. Granted, the view ain't bad, but I know he earns every damp, wrinkled dollar bill he makes.)

After surveying the territory for a bit, I decided I'd try and settle in Key West, and told Patrick as much. In my heart, though, all I wanted to do was get wasted—and stay that way. And Key West is the perfect place for that. There's a bar on almost every corner. Shit, there's a reason Jimmy Buffett owns both a nightclub and a music studio here—it seems like every person in town, tourist or local, is searchin for their lost shaker of salt.

Patrick had a spare room, and he told me it was mine; all I had to do was find a job and start paying rent *immediately*. So I started "looking" for a job, which really meant walking down the block, then sitting on a bench for hours, smoking cigarettes and watching people live their lives. That month-long period was one of the low points of my entire life; I was lonely, discouraged, frustrated, and running out of reasons to wake up in the morning.

Pat's house was on Truman Street, half a block from the Duval Street strip. (If you're unfamiliar, Duval Street is...well, if Bourbon Street and the San Diego beachfront boardwalk had a kid, it would be the Duval scene.) Even though some world-famous bars were mere feet away, I didn't want to go to them. For one, because of my disability, when I get drunk I'm a friggin *mess*. I can't walk, my speech is unintelligible, I piss myself every half-hour...you get the idea. So I didn't want to be "that guy" in public.

More important, though, was that I was alone in my race to oblivion. I wanted to get as numb as I could, as *fast* as I could, and I didn't want anybody else around to remind me of everything I was missing out on. So, as often as I could—or at least until my disability check was gone—after Patrick left for work I'd hobble down the street to the liquor store. Three hours or so later...nothingness.

It didn't take long for Pat to get wind of what was going on. He had a small fridge on the back patio where he kept beer—unlike me, he could have two or three and call it a night—and more than once, I (sort of) remember getting an angry text from him when he got home from work to find the fridge empty, and me dead drunk in bed. (I'd crawled out there and drunk them all, of course.)

The worst thing that happened was the night he came home to find me passed out on the living room floor. I was lying in a puddle of my own urine, and there was a big hole in the wall where I'd fallen and hit it with my head.

The next day Pat told me that I *had* to get help, or I would probably die, and that I couldn't live with him. At one point during that conversation, he wondered aloud what had happened to the happy, carefree, *responsible* John he'd known twenty years before...and it was like I felt something *snap* inside. (Probably my heart.) It was then I knew that after years and years of sinking, I'd finally found the bottom.

****

Several days later, Pat took me to a place here in Key West called the Neece Center, run by the Florida Keys Outreach Coalition. The program had three phases, I learned: Phase

One was a shelter for homeless men, with an emphasis on recovery from drugs and alcohol. (Phases Two and Three are continuations of that, are much nicer since they're in apartments in another part of town, and are for guys who want or need some long-term help.) It wasn't an ideal situation, but it was what I could afford. And it was a place to get sober—that's all I cared about.

"Patterson House"—that was its nickname since it was on Patterson Street—was divided into two dorm-style sleeping quarters, with five bunk beds in each room, a common area, and a full kitchen. As I settled in, I was surprised to learn that my shelter-mates were from all walks of life. The first guy who befriended me was a previously homeless veteran named Jimmy, who had a gimpy leg and only one eye. Jimmy kept me sane those first few nights, telling me stories of how he got arrested in Miami for getting in a fight with a gang of Cuban midgets—I'm not making that up—and how many homeless people in South Florida die because they pick the wrong place to sleep and get eaten by gators.

Twice a week, we had house meetings to go over program rules and regulations for the new guys. (And there were *always* new guys. I divided the men there into two groups: those who truly had a desire to sober up and get their shit together, and assholes who just wanted a bed for a few nights until they got enough money for another bottle of Smirnoff.)

One of the program requirements—and in retrospect, here's where I first realized God was running the show—was that we attend daily 12-Step meetings. So it was on April 5 that I first walked through the door to a meeting of Alcoholics Anonymous. I'd been to AA before, when I was in rehab about 15 years ago, so I knew the basics of the program, but it obviously hadn't worked for me back then.

The meeting was one of five daily AA meetings in a clubhouse called Anchors Aweigh. The clubhouse is an *awesome* facility, with several meeting rooms, a coffee bar, and a nice garden out back. I spent many hours in the garden, learning how to exist as a sober man.

I consider myself truly blessed that I had a lot of willingness to "work the program," as we AA's say, from the very start. For one, when I'd been home the previous Christmas, my mom had seen what sad shape I was in, and told me that I "needed to make some major changes in my life." (Understatement of the century right there.) I was just sick of living the way I was living, so I was an open vessel.

I decided to swallow my pride and do as others suggested. I went to *at least* one meeting every day, and soaked up the information like a sponge. One of the central ideas that a lot of AA newcomers struggle with is that of a Higher Power. One thing I know now—and the AA literature repeats this *ad finitum*—is that pretty much without exception, not one person can stay sober on his or her own. God simply *has* to be a part of the journey.

Like others, that was my biggest obstacle to overcome. I had grown up in a small Southern town, where of course religion—specifically Southern Baptist Christianity—ruled everybody. I saw what I considered a lot of religious hypocrisy during my formative years, so as I got older I developed a disdain for organized religion of *any* flavor. I considered myself spiritual, but not religious at all.

And thank *God*, pun definitely intended, that spirituality is an AA cornerstone. I knew in my heart that I wanted to change, and I knew that God would help me do that. But I refused to pray to the "God" that had told me it was a sin to go to my high school dance, or that had allowed one of the church deacons to get a DUI on a Sunday morning with his wife and three kids in the car.

But it didn't take me long to find God—MY God, who is not an invisible man in the sky, living on a cloud, with a list of things you should or shouldn't do. Simply put, my God is the force of good that lives within each person. And once I came to that simple understanding, I was transformed. I found a fantastic AA sponsor, L_____, who has been helping me through the 12 Steps. Steps 4-8, especially, were particularly cathartic, since they involve laying out all your shortcomings, and being honest with yourself about your moral standing. Purging those demons made me whole again.

****

Among other things, my sobriety has allowed me to move quickly through the FKOC program; I'm living in the third (and final) phase, which is a sober-living house I share with about fifteen other guys. I recently made some long-overdue changes to my Social Security Disability funding, and the process was extremely maddening. But I did it with the calmness of Buddha. The obsession to drink has been lifted; I spend my days with other sober, mature people...something that's literally a first for me.

When I tell people I'm getting sober in Key West, the usual response is something like, "Sober in Key West, huh? Wow, good luck with *that*!!" I always correct them with some tried-and-true logic: Since drinking is so prevalent here, it's out of necessity that the AA program is strong here, too.

That's the logic part. Now let me get busy about faith: As I build my relationship with God—MY God, remember—I realize how little control I've had over my life. I used to think that all the bad stuff that's happened to me, happened because I'm just a bad person.

But you know what? I now know that's not the case. Life's a journey, and everything that happens—good AND bad—is a lead-in to now. *Right* now, as I sit here typing.

God built me to be a happy person. He helped me survive getting beaten almost to death. He's allowed my life to be filled with almost non-stop laughter. And God had me drink uncontrollably for three decades so that I would come to Key West. I'm being healed here. And He put me here so that I can help people who are where I once was; so I can say, "That happened to me, and I got through it. You can too."

But most of all, He's made me feel proud when I declare: "My name is John, and I'm an alcoholic."

ACKNOWLEDGEMENTS:

I finally did it, Mom!!!

First, a huge thank-you to Kari Pope—editor, advisor, inspiration, genius, and the love of my life. Without you this book wouldn't exist. I love you, sweetness.

Thanks also to some great friends who have given me their opinions about the creative process: Dusty, Mike D, Cary and Chris, Chad Stewart, Patrick, and Natalie.

And a HUGE shout-out to all you folks from Facebook-land, who've read and given me your feedback on these stories over the past several years.

I love you all!

29514571R00117

Made in the USA
Charleston, SC
15 May 2014